ABC OF ACTION LEARNING

The Mike Pedler Library
Developing people and organizations
General Editor: Dr Mike Pedler

Books published simultaneously in this series:

Reg Revans
ABC of Action Learning

Nancy M. Dixon
Dialogue at Work

Mike Pedler and Kath Aspinwall
A Concise Guide to the Learning Organization

Rennie Fritchie and Malcolm Leary
Resolving Conflicts in Organizations

Would you like to receive regular information about forthcoming new books in the Mike Pedler Library? Would you like to send us your comments about the book you have read? If so, we would be very pleased to hear from you.

Lemos & Crane
20 Pond Square
Highgate Village
London N6 6BA
England
Tel   +44(0)181 348 8263
Fax   +44(0)181 347 5740
Email admin@lemos.demon.co.uk

ABC of Action Learning

Reg Revans

Lemos&Crane

This edition first published in Great Britain 1998
Lemos & Crane
20 Pond Square
Highgate Village
London N6 6BA

ISBN 1-898001-42-1

A CIP catalogue record for this book is available from the British Library.

Designed and typeset by DAP Ltd, London
Printed and bound by Redwood Books, Trowbridge

Contents

INTRODUCTION TO THE LIBRARY

"All learning is for the sake of action, and all action for the sake of friendship." John Macmurray

At the end of centuries and especially millennia, all manner of prophecies break out and gain hold in the public imagination. The world of business and management is no exception to this law as it entertains a great variety of excited ideas for dealing with the better ordering of business and corporate affairs in the face of the supposed end of certainty and, with this, the arts of prediction and strategic planning. In their place we are offered notions of paradox, of chaos and boundlessness, of multiple dilemmas and complexity theory. And these are merely at the "softer" end; at the other there is much old wine in new bottles as the nostrums of Taylorism and Fordism suffuse the apparently novel re-engineering and quality movements.

The value of learning

To be responsive to change, a child, adult, organization, even a society, must be adept at learning. Learning is the means not only of acquiring new knowledge and skill but also of making sense of our lives - individually and collectively - in increasingly fragmented times. We may not know "the how" of this or that, but we can go on hopefully in pursuit of learning a way through. In the absence of a plan, a blueprint for success, we can learn our way forward, growing in confidence as to what we can do and in who we are, making our own path.

For organizations, with an average lifespan of 40 years and declining, learning has become essential for survival

(De Geus). Organizational learning has also been suggested as the only sustainable source of competitive advantage (Senge) and the single most important quality which can be developed and traded (Garratt).

At community or society level new efforts at collaborative action and learning in public forums to tackle the "wicked" problems of poverty, inequality, pollution, crime and public safety look so much more relevant than the old questions of left or right, public or private, electoral democracy or entrepreneurial leadership.

For societies, communities, organizations and individuals the questions are similar: how can we develop those things which we do best so as to be able to trade, exchange, learn, whilst not shutting our eyes to the downsides, shadows, problems and consequences? How can we release energy, potential, self-reliability and active citizenship and build wealth, well-being, collective security, welfare, public services and generally improve the quality of our lives?

A Learning Society?

In an era characterised by large organizations and complexity, it has become plain that individual learning, however impressive, cannot alone resolve problems in relationships - be they at personal, team or organizational level. Equally, it is becoming clear that even the very best of our organizations, private or public, cannot alone resolve the intractable issues of communities and societies. The idea of the "learning organization" is a recognition of, and one response to, the limits of individual learning. But more is needed; there are urgent tasks to hand which go beyond the scope and remit of any single organization or coalition of agencies. As touched on above, these issues demand the organization of action and learning in a different context, and one which is scarcely yet glimpsed, yet alone grasped. In such an ideal collaboration as a Learning Society, there is:

- The freedom to learn - or not to learn - for individuals.

- An organizational aim to support the learning of all members and stakeholders and a desire to transform the organization, as a whole and when appropriate, in creating new products, services and relationships.

- A social drive to provide equality of opportunity for learning to all citizens, at least partly in order that they might contribute to that society being a good place to live in.

The links in this collaborative ideal can be represented diagramatically as follows:

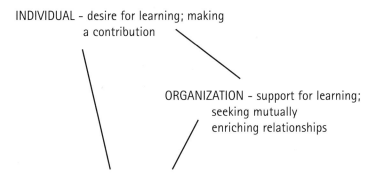

INDIVIDUAL - desire for learning; making a contribution

ORGANIZATION - support for learning; seeking mutually enriching relationships

COMMUNITY/SOCIETY - equal opportunities for learning; providing a good place to live

This manifesto is of course a re-interpretation of old revolutionary aspirations - Liberty (for individuals), the ruling value of Fraternity for organizations, and a duty of Equality of treatment and opportunity in the social sphere.

To each of these we hope to make a contribution, without being confined or encompassed by ideas of personal self-development, or of organizational change, learning, and transformation, nor yet by those of community development or social policy. If a book focuses on, say, organizational processes, then it also keeps an eye on the personal and social development aspects; if it is primarily aimed at the self-development of individuals, then this is in the context of working in organizations and living in society.

The books in the Library are concerned with learning and action on such pressing issues facing us as people working in organizations, living in communities, cities and societies. And whilst there is no single philosophy here, there is an implied criticism of the economic and cultural consensus which underlies much business and management literature in particular. There are challenges here for those who tend to assume that our future rests on the "roll out" of global, information-based capitalism supported by the spread of liberalism and democracy. There is support here for those who question whether individual or organizational development aimed at "high performance" or "excellence" inevitably leads only to desirable outcomes. Here, the irony of the self-proclaimed "learning organization" that is still not a healthy place for people to work in or to live next to, is noted. Here is an aspiration to engage our "best and brightest" and our talent for organizing with some of the really difficult and intractable issues facing us. Above all, we seek to be inclusive and to sustain and support all those trying to learn new things in order to act differently in pursuit of friendship.

Beyond ideas to useful action

Because action and learning require more than just good ideas, the Library is characterised by two more "laws of three". In terms of content, each book contains:

- *educational input* - ideas of substance that you need to know about.

- *invitations to action* - at various points it is suggested that you need to stop and to actually do something with the ideas in order to learn.

- *ethical or political elements* - being an honest colleague, doing the "right thing", seeking good purposes or responding to difficult tasks and circumstances usually imply ethical dilemmas or struggle and perhaps the need for moral support in action and learning.

In terms of pitch or level, though they aim to be attractive and accessible, these books are not "easy reads". Not content with theories and suspicious of easy answers, tools and techniques, these books offer a middle ground of active methods and approaches to the problems and questions posed. Here is an invitation to self-confrontation for the reader. Aware of the complexity and of the questions to which there are no answers, nevertheless there are ways forward, structures to use, directions to follow in order to engage your own energies, the ingenuity of colleagues and the aspirations of customers or those you serve in order to learn your way through. You can't put such a book down without at least thinking of doing something differently.

MIKE PEDLER

EDITORIAL PREFACE

This edition of the *ABC of Action Learning* follows two previous ones, the 1978 original published with the help of the Forward Engineering Group Training Scheme in Birmingham, England and the bigger 1983 version (referred to in the Bibliography below). This third edition keeps closely to the actual text of the latter except for changes and additions noted below. These changes may seem quite extensive, and I have worried over them.

The main deletions from the 1983 edition are the five pages (section 2) of Chapter 2 "Managerial Levels and Action Learning Exchange Options" and the five page Chaper 6 "Some Illustrations of Action Learning Programmes". The former is an excursion into the four project options based on the Belgian full-time exchange model whilst the latter covers the ground only until 1983. It was difficult to update these sections without completely new text and after considerable thought I decided to leave them out.

The main additions to the 1983 edition are a new Chapter 8 "The Enterprise as a Learning System" (taken from *The Origins and Growth of Action Learning*, Chapter 26 pp.280-286, see Bibliography, below); an extra page at the end of Chapter 7, including a 14 item list of design issues that appeared in the first edition but not in the second, and a new Bibliography for which I am entirely responsible.

I have added "The Enterprise as a Learning System" (written in 1969) because it addresses the issue of the learning organization well before its recent popularity. Revans has always envisaged Action Learning in this wider context in contrast to those who present it as a small group learning method. The new Bibliography is in three parts; firstly a review of four of Revans' most important books, then a listing of another 15 of his works with shorter comments and finally 14 briefly annotated books by other writers on Action Learning. The list of design issues in Chapter 7 is useful and I don't know why it was previously dropped.

Other changes concern the actual written text where I wanted to improve "readability". Revans' liking for long sentences, with multiple semi-colons in lengthy paragraphs, achieves a magnificent but dense oratorical style, which can be hard to penetrate for all but the most persevering reader. I have shortened sentences and paragraphs, altered some chapter and section titles, put more "white space" into the layout and changed some terms, for example, "colleague" or "participant" for "fellow"; "staff" for "subordinates"; "whatever" for "whatsoever"; "whoever" for "whomsoever" and so on. All of this is controversial; this interfering with the voice of the man described by Alistair Mant as a giant, one of the "very few names of real distinction in management education".

I asked Reg to adjudicate on this exercise of editorial licence but he has more important things to do than police manuscripts. His blessing is more likely to fall on all those who not only read but also who get on and do something about it.

MIKE PEDLER

FOREWORD BY DR DAVID BOTHAM

In 1637, a French philosopher by the name of Descartes wrote these words:

> *"I was brought up on letters from my childhood; and since it was urged upon me that by means of them one could acquire clear and assured knowledge of all that is useful in life, I was extremely eager to learn them. But as soon as I had finished the whole course of studies at the end of which one is normally admitted to the ranks of the learned, I completely altered my opinion. For I found myself embarrassed by so many doubts of error, that it seemed to me that the only profit I had had from my efforts to acquire knowledge was the progressive discovery of my own ignorance."*

I find Descartes' conclusion remarkable in the sense that it not only echoes the minds of other great thinkers but that the text could have been written by the author of this particular book. Although this was written for a different period of European history, learning from one's own ignorance still remains the greatest of all developmental stimuli. To suggest that Action Learning is as simple as ABC or the "letters from one's childhood" is an interesting thought; to discover its fundamental challenge to our understanding of the process nature of human learning through the discovery of ignorance is an even more interesting thought.

At first glance it can easily be assumed that Revans' *ABC of Action Learning* is a work for managers on how to manage the yet undiscovered challenges of tomorrow. But on careful reading the book is speaking to everyone who is engaged in improving professional practice and in the encouragement of fellow human beings in the pursuance of tolerant understanding. So, in some ways this *ABC of Action Learning* is a succinct philosophical text that emphasises the examination of one's learning by deliberately putting such learning into action so one can learn indefinitely.

Such a work can be viewed as an attack on conventional and formal education that prides itself on providing answers, solutions and explanations organized within a teaching syllabus. But I would encourage the reader of this book to look beyond this assumption and consider the tremendous opportunities for both teacher and student when one's work becomes a "syllabus of learning". This is why Revans goes beyond the convention of teaching knowledge or 'P' as he symbolises it, and introduces what good philosophers and scientists have always done, that is subject their knowledge of 'P' to fresh and tough questions or 'Q'. This way of penetrating one's understanding of something by introducing new questions removes the limitations of one's learning capacity and alleviates one's knowledge of one's own learning process.

Revans is in no doubt that a major part of our society's current problems is inextricably linked to the way we perceive and organize our education in linear methods built around our over obsession with facts thrust upon the involuntary minds of students by experts. He argues that observable behavioural change only takes place when learners decide for themselves and when they have been faced with real issues. This is why Revans begins his book by stating, "There can be no learning without action and no action without learning."

Simple stuff you might exclaim! Didn't Confucius link understanding to doing or action in 500 BC and didn't Roger Bacon associate learning with change in the 13th century? Indeed, and Revans would be the first to agree with such conclusions, claiming that he was not the inventor of Action Learning. But he certainly did pioneer the approach by explaining the process in an outstandingly courageous way, yet avoiding the temptation to produce a prescriptive manual or textbook concerned with the teaching of Action Learning.

The first publication of the text came out in 1978, which Revans introduced as a "collection of ideas" drawn from his experience of working with various forms of Action Learning. He preferred to view his origional version as "a box of paints, filled with concentrated colours for composing various patterns of Action Learning." This third and revised edition of the *ABC of Action Learning* recreates some of the patterns of the Action Learning process so that Revans' ideas and theories are clear and accessible within the resurgence of Action Learning in the UK and elsewhere. To my mind this edition reasserts what Descartes said over 350 years ago,

> *"the reading of good books is like a conversation with the best men of past centuries; in fact like a prepared conversation in which they reveal only the best of their thoughts."*

DR DAVID BOTHAM
Director of the Revans Centre for Action Learning and Research at the University of Salford.

Dedicated to Janet Barbara Craig whose support made
Action Learning possible in the country of its origin.

THERE CAN BE NO LEARNING WITHOUT ACTION AND NO ACTION WITHOUT LEARNING

"To do a little good is better than to write difficult books. The perfect man is nothing if he does not diffuse benefits on others, if he does not console the lonely. The way of salvation is open to all, but know that a man deceives himself if he thinks he can escape his conscience by taking refuge in a monastery. The only remedy for evil is healthy reality."

Buddha, Benares Deer Park, 518 BC

"One must learn by doing the thing; for though you think you know it you have no certainty, until you try."

Sophocles, Trachiniae, 415 BC

"But be does of the word, and not only hearers of it, blinding yourselves with false ideas. Because if any man is a hearer of the word and not a doer, he is like a man looking at his natural face in a glass; for after looking at himself he goes away, and in a short time he has no memory of what he was like. But he who goes on looking into the true law which makes him free, being not a hearer without memory but a doer putting it into effect, this man will have a blessing on his acts."

Letter of St James, chapter 1 verses 22-25, AD 60

"It is not enough to know what is good; you must be able to do it."

George Bernard Shaw, 'Back to Methuslah' Act IV, scene 1, AD 1921

"All meaningful knowledge is for the sake of action, and all meaningful action for the sake of friendship."

John Macmurray, *The Self As Agent*, AD 1953

1. The Characteristic Assumptions of Action Learning

IN THIS CHAPTER: Twenty assumptions about management, learning and the nature of knowledge, summarised under the prime idea of Action Learning; many of these assumptions have long been accepted by others.

Contents

1 The Characteristic Assumptions of Action Learning

In any epoch of rapid change those organizations unable to adapt are soon in trouble. Adaptation is achieved only by learning, namely, by being able to do tomorrow that which might have been unnecessary today, or to be able to do today what was unnecessary last week.

PROGRAMMED KNOWLEDGE

The organization that continues to express only the ideas of the past is not learning, and training systems intended to develop our young may do little more than to make them proficient in yesterday's technique. Thus learning cannot be solely the acquisition of new programmed knowledge, howsoever important the possession of that knowledge may be. When none can say what the morrow shall bring forth, none can tell what stock of programmed propositions is most economically applicable; the teaching institutions can do no more than offer their own selections.

But all managers will be caught up by the currents of change, and swept into new unknowns never before encountered, let alone lived through and explored. In such conditions, nobody can say what programmed knowledge those in such predicaments may need, since their first obligation will be to search what they are able to perceive as their new environment.

In such exploration of the unfamiliar too great a reliance upon inappropriate programmed knowledge may become a fatal weakness: the idolisation of the past has been the downfall of countless traditions – and a tradition on its deathbed may be guaranteed to deflect attention from what is killing it. So it is that the subjective aspects of searching the unfamiliar, or of learning to pose useful and discriminating questions in conditions of ignorance, risk and confusion, must become as well understood, and as effectively employed, by managers as are all the syllabuses of programmed instruction.

THE LEARNING EQUATION

Action Learning takes up from the start the need to help managers – and all others who engage in management – acquire this insight into the posing of questions by the simple device of setting them to tackle real problems that have so far defied solution. We may structure our argument from the outset by identifying the acquisition of programmed knowledge as P, and of questioning insight as Q, so writing the Learning Equation as:

$$L = P + Q$$

In this, our principal interest is in Q, the idea of action learning. We do not reject P; it is the stuff of traditional instruction.

★

The inalienable assumptions of Action Learning

programmes – twenty in all – are set out below. Procedural recommendations, or logistics, follow next in Chapter 2.

LEARNING IS CRADLED IN THE TASK

The primary occupation of managers is to treat their problems (or to seize their opportunities) and these may be defined as the conditions that either obstruct or advance the attainment of their goals. Managers, in other words, must make up their minds about what to do and settle for doing it. All secondary activity should be linked as closely as possible to this everyday task.

For this simple reason, Action Learning is cradled in the very task itself, asking whether that task can be done so that, merely by reflecting upon how it currently seems to be done, the very doing of it supplies the learning generally offered far from the scenes of managerial activity.

FORMAL INSTRUCTION IS NOT SUFFICIENT

This does not imply that Action Learning rejects all formal instruction (P). It merely recognises that such instruction, aimed at imparting what is normally known to others and often classified in such ways as to test by written examination how much has been imparted, cannot of itself stimulate the posing of insightful questions (Q) in other fields altogether, of which some may be so ill-defined as to suggest, at the outset, no branch of programmed knowledge worth exploring.

On the contrary, Action Learning recognises that, in the absence of such insight, the use to which a wealth of programmed knowledge may be put is limited. That which may be known cannot be applied until insightful questions have been asked; P may be necessary, but, in the absence of Q, cannot be sufficient. As was said by a distinguished authority: "Think not that I am come to destroy the law, or the prophets; I am not come to destroy, but to fulfil." (*Matthew* ch.5 v.17)

PROBLEMS REQUIRE INSIGHTFUL QUESTIONS

Traditional instruction (P) prepares for the treatment of *puzzles*, or difficulties from which escapes are thought to be known (troubles with programmed solutions), even although the escape or solution may be hard to discover, and calls for the skill of experts. Action Learning, on the other hand, deals with the resolution of *problems* (and the acceptance of *opportunities*) about which no single course of action is to be justified by any code of programmed knowledge, so that different managers, all reasonable, experienced and sober, might set out by treating them in markedly different ways.

Problems and opportunities are treated by leaders who must be aware of their own value systems, differing between individuals, and of the influences of their past personal experiences. These will strongly influence their subjective judgments and, hence, their predisposing willingness to take risks. Such risks are diminished to the extent that further discriminating questions are posed and answered; this demands *exploratory insight* (Q).

LEARNING INVOLVES DOING

Managerial learning implies an ability to carry out the solution of the problem as well as to specify that solution. The difference is more subtle than is often understood, otherwise case methods, business games and the like would scarcely have been so long at work to bring management education to its present condition.

The confusion tends to arise because so much managerial action is necessarily an exchange of words (issue of instructions, agreement to pay, approval of measure, and so forth) that the distinctions between getting something done and talking about getting it done may be simply overlooked. However this may be, there is an observable difference between consulting past reports of the Olympic Games to decide that one may need to clear two metres forty to win the next high jump, on the one hand, and, on the other, actually sailing over that height before the crowd in the stadium. It is likewise not enough that the manager should be able to specify such-and-such a way of resolving their difficulty; he or she must be able to effectuate it as part of their contractual mission.

LEARNING IS VOLUNTARY

Any person, whether manager or not, changes their observable behaviour, or learns in the sense in which that word is used here, only if they wish to do so.

One learns, or changes one's behaviour, of one's own volition and not at the will of others (unless under duress, bribery or other influences, which are not inspirations to learning in the sense here implied). Moreover, one may be cognitively aware of a need to behave differently and yet remain determined not to do so in practice. This is often the consequence of inadequate self-understanding, when the subject either does not know what they believe in, or, more profoundly, has not grasped the concept of belief.

URGENT PROBLEMS OR ENTICING OPPORTUNITIES PROVIDE THE SPUR FOR LEARNING

The menace of urgent problems, or the lure of enticing opportunities, are likely to reinforce a desire to learn, should behavioural change – or even fresh belief – be called for to clear up the problems or to bring forward the opportunities.

ACTION AND FEEDBACK

In learning such new behaviour, persons must attack real problems, preferably ill defined, or fertile opportunities, howsoever remote, in such manners as to remain continuously aware of their progress and of the influences determining that progress. In scientific jargon, any system that is to learn, whether an individual manager or a national cabinet, must regularly receive and interpret inputs about its own outputs.

THE RISK IMPERATIVE

These attacks, whether upon problems or upon opportunities, must carry significant risk of penalty for failure.

Those who are not obliged to assess the risk to themselves of pursuing, or of trying to pursue, such-and-such lines of action cannot, by their indifference to the outcome, explore their own value systems nor identify any trustworthy pattern of their own beliefs. Non-risk exercises, such as case discussions, often motivated by exhibitionism or a need for social approval, may draw from some participants declarations of belief that, while not misleading those who hear them, can help only to deceive those who express them. Even U.S. educators, such as Argyris, now criticise the case method.

LEARNING AS RE-INTERPRETING PAST EXPERIENCE

Lasting behavioural change is more likely to follow the reinterpretation of past experiences than the acquisition of fresh knowledge. Among senior managers, in particular, it is in re-reading what is already scribbled on the cortical slate that leads to changed behaviour, rather than in copying out new messages upon it.

THE CONTRIBUTION OF PEERS

Such re-interpretations of past experience, being necessarily subjective, complex and ill-structured, are more likely to be intelligible through exchanges with other managers themselves anxious to learn by re-ordering their own perceptions than through discussions with non-managers (including teachers of management) not exposed to real risk in responsible action.

THE CENTRAL IMPORTANCE OF THE SET

In consequence, managers readily learn to accept and to discharge their real-life responsibilities by contrived exchanges with other managers during the prosecution of real-life activities. They learn both to give to and to accept from other managers the criticism, advice and support needful to develop their own managerial powers, all in the course of identifying and treating their own personal tasks.

This is the argument for the centrality of the 'set' that is the cutting edge of every Action Learning programme, by whatever variety of names such programmes are now becoming known. It is particularly important that the set is kept mainly to the reporting, analysis and planning of real-time action continually being taken by the participants in their operational backgrounds.

So-called sets that meet to exchange feeling and opinions not immediately derived from a current undertaking to change some reality observable to others may be justified as 'sensitivity training', as an 'encounter group', and as a dozen other modish rituals. Unless, however, its discussions are based on the verifiable evidence of deliberated achievement it may be little more than an efficient (and expensive) means of replacing one set of misconceptions for another. Since it is easy to run, it will be widely on offer.

THE PLACE OF EXPERTISE

The undue intervention of experts carrying no personal responsibility for the real-life actions that bring the set together is, at best, ambiguous; in general, opinionative; and, at worst, reactionary.

In Action Learning, as it is now accepted, expert advice (P), once the need for it has been defined, is increasingly sought from other participants (primarily interested to develop their own personal Q). In most programmes there is a sufficient access to P through the Q-seekers and their friends to make the ad hoc intervention of experts unnecessary. The quest for Q, indeed, becomes more fruitful when a participant is able to understand, by supplying another participant with P, how their colleague perceived that a quota of P was needed.

THE RESPONSIBILITY OF MANAGEMENT TEACHERS

The responsibility of management teachers in the development of Action Learning is to contrive, with those managers themselves and those with whom those same managers normally work, the conditions in which they may learn with and from each other by the exchanges described above.

It is particularly vital that these conditions respect the need for the management teachers themselves to learn from such contrivings. Only if their involvement is manifestly a learning experience for teachers of management subjects, helping them from the comments of the real-life managers to see more clearly the relevance of their programmed knowledge (P) to the solution of the problems on which participants are engaged, should such specialists be offered a continuing attachment to a set. Even this role for the professional teacher, all the same, is less satisfactory than to allow her or him to become a Q-seeking participant to tackle a project quite independent of all pre-disposing P knowledge.

LEARNING WITH AND FROM EACH OTHER

Exactly as managerial learning is a social exchange in which managers learn with and from each other during the diagnosis and treatment of real problems (and opportunities), so may teachers of management learn together, with either managers or other teachers.

This can be done by tackling the design, introduction, conduct and review of Action Learning programmes and by regularly meeting in sets intended from the outset to monitor what is going on in the substantive activities of the managers at work on the real-life problems and opportunities. This may be seen as Action Learning of the second order, or Action Learning to improve Action Learning, rather than, say, patient care or factory costs.

THE FACILITATOR ROLE

To launch the set quickly into its discussions (and so to conserve the time of its participant managers), there may be a need when it is first formed for some supernumerary.

Such a combiner, brought in to speed the integration of the set must contrive that it achieves independence of them at the earliest possible moment, and open discussions between the substantive members of the set and the supernumerary to plan this should be pursued without embarrassment. It is vital that Action Learning takes advantage of our present disillusion with the academy to escape yet another round of dependence upon ambiguous facilitators. It may well be that, in the near future, any help to get fresh sets underway can be adequately provided by managers now participating in action learning sets as substantive members.

LEARNING IS MEASURED BY THE RESULTS OF ACTION

The success, or otherwise, of the managers as they work upon their real-life problems or opportunities is to be assessed solely by their applications to practice, whether in the phases of diagnosis, prescription or therapy.

It is particularly important that the interpretation of what is going on by discussion within the set is not unduly influenced by non-involved facilitators – one school of which is now advocating freedom from real-life involvement, a step back to the case discussion method run by star faculty who know the case. Only continuous comparison between prediction of outcome and observation of actual result, made week after week at the set meeting, will bring home to its members the nature of their learning sequences and the five stages of which those sequences are composed.

FRESH QUESTIONS

The allocation to each participant of a real-life exercise that is ill-structured and obscure from the outset (and for which there can be no preconceived line of attack) must encourage in each of them an ability to seek for, and to identify, those fresh questions likely to open up promising avenues of enquiry.

Participants become encouraged to explore what they cannot see around them as well as what they imagine they can, and in this vital mapping of their own ignorance they are encouraged by their colleagues in the set. The essence of Action Learning is to pose increasingly insightful questions from an origin of ignorance, risk and confusion. This quest for insight (Q) complements expert drill (P).

THE CYCLE OF ACTION LEARNING AND RESEARCH

The structure of the approach to experimental investigation known as the *scientific method* – as distinct from dialectic and sophistry – identifies five successive stages (observation, provisional hypothesis, trial, audit and review) and is identical to those of:

- the *rational decision* (survey, first decision, pilot run, evaluation and final decision);
- the *learning sequence* (awareness of ignorance, new idea, taking a chance, watching effect, remembering for next time); and
- the *advisory argument*, either given or received (admission of need, choice of counsel, test of confidence by action, estimate of outcome, confirmation – or rejection – of counsel).

The deliberated diagnosis, prescription and therapy associated with Action Learning thus makes (a) deciding, (b) learning, and (c) advising all three aspects of the same essential and logical process – the application of the scientific method to changing real systems managed by real people.

This simple analysis suggests that the distinctions drawn by academics between research, action, learning and communication are highly artificial, if not knowingly misconceived. There can be no action without learning, and no learning without action.

THE MULTIPLIER EFFECT

Since in management systems learning must involve more than one person, in that whoever questions what goes on around them must also raise questions in the minds of others, an Action Learning programme will cause not only the set members to learn, but also those in the fields of the projects upon which the substantive members are engaged.

In some programmes this multiplying effect will equal, or even exceed, that of the set exchanges in the value of the managerial learning to which it gives rise.

THE OBJECTIVES OF ACTION LEARNING

Action Learning necessarily has three major objectives, and it is idle to design programmes intended to concentrate on one of them. None can be accomplished unless its two counterparts are also encouraged. They are to:

1 Make useful progress upon the treatment of some problem or opportunity in the real world.

2 Give nominated managers (and many others within the operational fields of the problems or opportunities on which they will work) sufficient scope, variable but sustained, to learn for themselves, and in the company of colleagues, how best to approach ill-structured challenges to which nobody can, at the outset, suggest any satisfactory response.

3 Encourage teachers and others in management development to perceive their missions afresh. They should no longer try to teach managers

anything about how to manage, but should see themselves as having to contrive, with senior managements, the conditions in which all managers, including those at the top, learn with and from each other in the pursuit of their common and everyday duties.

These three objectives are to Action Learning what the three sides are to a triangle, essential to its character and incompatible with the suggestion that any one of them can be greater than the sum of the other two.

★

THE FUNDAMENTAL NATURE OF ACTION LEARNING

This coda to the first chapter has little to do with any programme of Action Learning, but our review of the subject, however condensed it is supposed to be, would suffer by its omission. It has therefore been included to demonstrate that the argument above (to relate learning, advising and deciding by assimilating them all to the scientific method, and forming a broad statement of rational behaviour called Action Learning) is in the very nature of things, like Pythagoras' theorem or the laws of electromagnetic induction.

The scientific method – the intellectual structuring of experience to achieve a command over the world – consists in five steps:

- *Observation or survey*: collecting and classifying reports of what seems to go on.
- *Theory or hypothesis*: suggesting causal relationships between those happenings.

- *Test or experiment*: carrying out activities dependent on those causal relationships.
- *Audit or review*: asking if those activities go as was expected.
- *Review or control*: rejecting, changing or accepting the causal relationships.

Personal relationships are referred to here solely in the grammatical sense of first, second and third person, something common to all languages by the nature of language itself: person(s) speaking, person(s) spoken to, and person(s) or thing(s) spoken about. Language may be taken as a model of awareness, too: awareness of self, awareness of companions, awareness of third parties and of external world.

It may also be taken as a model of influence: influence upon self, influence upon companions, and influence upon third parties and upon external world. These three may be seen as learning (changing self), advising (changing others), and deciding (action changing external world).

Since very few activities can be pursued in one-person-form alone, all three levels of the general model are necessarily involved. When the activity is rational it can be represented by Fig. 1 on p.18, which sets out the prime idea of Action Learning.

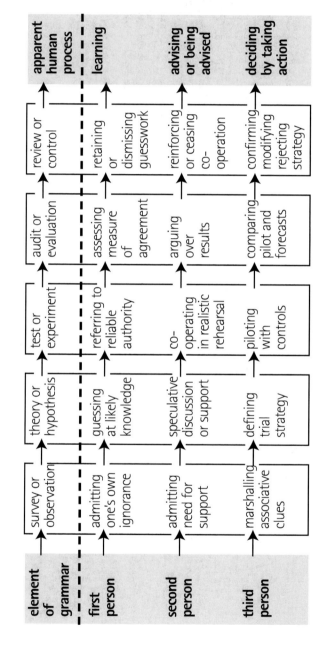

Fig 1. Five stage cycle of the scientific method

element of grammar	survey or observation	theory or hypothesis	test or experiment	audit or evaluation	review or control	apparent human process
first person	admitting one's own ignorance	guessing at likely knowledge	referring to reliable authority	assessing measure of agreement	retaining or dismissing guesswork	learning
second person	admitting need for support	speculative discussion or support	co-operating in realistic rehearsal	arguing over results	reinforcing or ceasing co-operation	advising or being advised
third person	marshalling associative clues	defining trial strategy	piloting with controls	comparing pilot and forecasts	confirming modifying rejecting strategy	deciding by taking action

2. Essential Logistics

IN THIS CHAPTER: Some operational forms assumed by Action Learning programmes, offered in the expectation that they will be copied and the hope that they will be improved upon.

Contents

2 Essential Logistics

The study of real life problems or opportunities by real managers in real time admits of a wide range of programme design. For example, those actively searching the fields in which fresh questions need to be posed (and, if possible, resolved) may do so either full or part-time. They may pursue their enquires alone or in small teams. They may remain in their own employing organization or they can be seconded elsewhere; they may even desert their own field of professional competence to find themselves working from first principles in some functional labyrinth they have entered for the first time in their lives - and, by doing so, they may also oblige the experts by whom they are now surrounded to think afresh about their unconscious assumption.

It is thus for the senior managements willing to try Action Learning as a medium of improvement to make up their minds about the logistical forms their programmes are to take, and this chapter suggests some of the details to which their attention must be given.

EXCHANGE OPTIONS

There are four principal exchange options for designing Action Learning programmes: (1) a familiar problem in a familiar setting; (2) a familiar problem in an unfamiliar setting; (3) an unfamiliar problem in a familiar setting; (4) an unfamiliar problem in an unfamiliar setting. These are discussed below.

A familiar problem in a familiar setting

A participant may examine afresh some aspect of his or her existing job, an option very popular with the chief executives of small enterprises forming sets to exchange ideas about their own strategic problems and, thereby, to bring the effects of each other's judgment and experience directly into the course of their own decisions.

There may be little in the way of physical transfer to some other work place, although, as their set exchanges (often starting as conversations over a series of dinner parties to which all play host in turn) open up new thoughts, they will consult their diaries to make visits to each others territories, even if each must remain, as before the programme was set up, almost wholly preoccupied with running their own business.

When a group in the same company gets engaged on its own problems at the points where these arise, we see what has become known as the Quality Circle - advocated in this country during the 1950s but unacceptable to the then-prevailing economic opinion that the future lay with the bigger enterprises run by those qualified in management science. (It is most important that new academic inbreedings, howsoever smooth and sophisticated, do not just replace the old, and that new manipulations of the familiar task in its familiar setting are not begun independently of action learning at the top. Q-Circles must always express the unique policies of the firm; bought in bulk as packages they may do harm.)

A familiar problem in an unfamiliar setting

A personnel officer from one enterprise may be invited to join those in some other concern trying to simplify (or otherwise improve) their wages structure. The visitor is not engaged as an expert to tell the host management how to set about the innovation they have in mind; but is there both to watch how colleagues interpret their own professional roles, especially as these bear upon other departments of the receiving organization, and, as time goes on, to test the validity of their own creative ideas, the ability to make them clear to colleague professionals and their powers of adaptation while temporarily freed from the habitual constraints of their own job back home.

The transferred personnel officer will become as much a true learner of his or her own potential as they may see themself at the outset as a qualified adviser. Only those experts who recognise a need to learn - and recognise it so clearly that they are anxious to accept the change of the exchange - should be encouraged to move. Those professionals who imagine they are being commissioned to go somewhere else in order to instruct those less able than themselves should not be allowed to menace what Action Learning has trouble enough already to get started.

An unfamiliar problem in a familiar setting

A production engineer, much concerned with the flow of work through his own factories, may join others in trying to rationalise the traditional wages structure now believed to be hindering the productive potential of the system by which he is also employed.

Perhaps the most recent and striking illustration of

this option is to be found in the Action Learning set established among the five directors of a large woodworking concern, over a hundred years old, but lately threatened with closure by its uncompetitive factory costs. Each director worked part-time on a major problem of some other department, thereby starting the examination and treatment of unfamiliar problems in familiar settings - since all stayed within their own firm - from the boardroom to the shop floor, finishing with 72 foremen/supervisors working in 12 sets each of six. Every member of every set looked into the operational troubles of some section of the works about which, to begin with, they knew nothing whatsoever. This collective effort, by reducing factory costs by 30 per cent and by enabling the main flow line to be reduced by two-thirds its previous length, preserved a thousand jobs under notice only twelve months before.

An unfamiliar problem in an unfamiliar setting

The regional manager of a large bank spends nine months full time in an oil company to ask what are the assumptions underlying its distribution policies, and the nature of the information on which those policies are implemented. The aim is to discover what manner of marketing system should be developed to make the best use of the cargoes arriving regularly at the company's refiner, so that the sales department can control what products the crude will supply to a greater extent than in the past, when, by long tradition, the distributors had to get rid of what the refinery engineers believed they could most economically turn out from the resources at their disposal.

As complementary to this exchange, the chief logistics and purchasing officer of the oil refinery also spends as much time within the bank to ask a similar question: does the bank need a marketing strategy? If so, how will those now running the bank determine what that strategy ought to be, and how will they restructure an organization, now more than one hundred years old, that has managed to get along without arousing the need for any clear definition of its place in the market?

INDIVIDUALS AND TEAMS

Action Learning programmes may equally well be formed for small teams to study real problems as for individual managers to be the participants. In the Hospitals Internal Communications Project, (see Bibliography below) small teams of doctor, nurse and administrator formed both the clients for the ten participating institutions and (with different persons) also the teams charged with the field studies (participants). In practice, they also involved many hundreds of the other staff in the hospitals as helpers, both in diagnosing the afflictions of the hospitals and in doing something to put things right.

Thus, with the variations of full-time and part-time engagement, and of individual and team field work, all with four main options in the allocation of projects, there is scope enough for fitting Action Learning to the resources of any organization with a mind to try it.

Sponsors, Clients, Client Groups, Participants

Sponsors

Every project offered by a participating enterprise believing itself to be faced with sufficient trouble (or opportunity) to wish to join an Action Learning programme must nominate a sponsor to the programme organisers who is ready to act on behalf of the participating enterprise should need arise.

The difficulties of persuading a score of firms to act together as a consortium will be unnecessarily multiplied if their representatives cannot be summoned quickly to deal with the unexpected. For example, when a number of the firms in the first Belgian programme were so impressed with the effects it was having upon their own management that they suggested their participants ought to have the chance of visiting the US in order to present their findings to the experts from its leading business schools and to the strategic planners of such companies as IBM, Exxon, AT & T, GE of America, and a dozen others in correspondence with the Belgian economy.

There is an immense advantage in forming close contacts between those in command of the separate participating concerns, not only for the speedy resolution of the unexpected, but also as a learning exercise for these very powerful businessmen themselves. The same may also be said for the teams in charge at the ten London hospitals. These generally consisted of the chairman of the hospital medical committee, the matron (chief nursing officer), and the hospital secretary or house governor. Such senior persons found many novel things to say to each other as the results of the studies set into motion across the floors of their hospitals were reported back to them - and, what is more, acted upon.

Clients

Every participating organization must also nominate a client for every project; he or she is usually that senior member of its staff more concerned than any other with ensuring that something is done about the project, both in clearing the way for its effective diagnosis and in preparing the management to give its recommendations a fair trial.

Clients from different enterprises also have the unrivalled opportunity to learn with and from each other by occasionally meeting, either by themselves or with their participants, to exchange interpretations of what seems to be going on. Since it is very common for the original project sent in by a prospective participant firm to be misconceived, and so to call for fundamental restructuring once the participant has started on their field diagnosis, it is essential to regard the first nomination of the client as provisional.

Client groups

As a course of action starts to build up following the field studies and their incorporation into a strategic plan, the client and the participant - as well as the sponsor - will soon recognise the need for allies to implement that plan. This calls for the recruitment of a client group, about which there is a further reference below.

Participants

The choice of suitable participants must, of course, lie with the sponsors, and much that is impossible here to specify will guide their choices, such as the personal qualities of prospective participants and the nature of the projects offered within the programme. It is useful to stress at this point that Action Learning programmes are not intended to communicate technical expertise in accounting, computer programming, quantitative methods, and the like. Applicants who build their cases upon their need or desire to seek technical qualifications should therefore have the true purpose of the programme explained to them, and ought not to be preferred to those who are more anxious to understand their own responses to conditions of risk, ignorance and confusion.

PROBLEMS, NOT PUZZLES

We repeat that Action Learning is not a satisfactory approach to resolving puzzles, or difficulties to which a solution clearly exists even if it is hard to find, such as the best way of reducing the time or cost of some specific operation (already examined to ensure quite unequivocally that this can be done without starting all manner of other unexpected objections, and is something that can be tackled by some work study engineer or cost accountant or similar specialist).

Action Learning is to make useful progress on the treatment of problems/opportunities, where no solution can possibly exist already because different managers, all honest, experienced and wise, will advocate different courses of action in accordance with their different value systems, their different past experiences and their different hopes for the future.

THE LEARNING EQUATION

The contrast between puzzles and problems, on the one hand, and between participants who are seeking techniques and those seeking to understand their own responses to uncertainty, on the other, emphasises the dual nature of true learning.

There is first the need to amass *programmed knowledge* (technical expertise, functional specialism) or the fruits of authoritarian instruction, here designated as P, and duly described at length in the syllabuses of teaching institutions of all kinds, from universities to training centres for the mentally disabled.

But then, especially today, there is the need to master the taking of decisions in circumstances of change so violent as to be confusing. This calls for an ability to pose useful questions when there can be no certainty as to what next might happen. This *questioning insight* we designate as Q; it is something quite different from P, and is exercised by leaders, while P is deployed by experts.

In the design of Action Learning programmes it is absolutely essential to make clear the distinction between P and Q, even if, in most of life's troubles, the manager is called on to exercise some of each. (If we denote learning by L, then $L = P + Q$: our equation.)

THE ESSENTIAL CHARACTER OF THE SET

Apart from working regularly upon their projects, under whatever variations of the exchange options set out above, each participant is to become a member regularly devoted to enkindle the meetings of the same set (group) of participants, between four and six in number, at which each gives to the others an account of their progress and their setbacks.

The set is the cutting edge of the Action Learning programme, and nothing must be allowed to stand in the way of the participants regular appearances at it. In practice, the participants themselves see that nothing ever does; (in an early programme run by GEC in Britain, out of a total of 732 participant attendances 729 were kept).

The detailed planning of the set meetings should be left to the participants, who will soon learn when what they have to say is likely to arouse the creative interest of their colleagues. These will ensure that no member of their set is allowed to coast along on the presentations of the others. All, with inexorable certitude, will be called upon to disclose much that they had for many years successfully hidden from themselves, such as what (if anything) they really believe in - for, should they not know this, they cannot decide what risks to take.

And this is the first need of the managerial policy maker - or why they say the things they say and do the things they do. At the end of the first major programme in Belgium, the question voted by all participants as the most important they had learned to ask themselves after nine months of self-disclosure to their colleagues was simply: "What is an honest man, and what need I do to become one?" (This can also be most profitably posed by several organizers of Action Learning programmes whose acquaintance I have made.)

INDUCTION EXERCISES

There is generally a need, before launching participants upon their projects, to help them with a brief induction course. The objectives include the following.

1 An explanation of what Action Learning is supposed to be

This is most readily framed around the learning equation set forth above, and stressing that it is to develop the capacity to ask fresh questions rather than to communicate technical knowledge.

Once it is clear that whatever technical knowledge any particular participant may need to get ahead with their project will be supplied on a personal level, the members of the set will devote themselves to their projects as a first resolve, and, as a second, offer to coach any other participant in the programme (and, by the end of the first month, any member of the directing staff) in the field of their own professional expertise.

Participants engaged on the analysis of real and difficult projects do not take long to discover the immense benefit to themselves of helping another with the technical codes that they believe themselves to have need of. It is helpful to bring this later development of the programme to the attention of the participants at the outset, since the prospect of such mutual support will help to consolidate the learning community.

2 To make the participants in some degree curious about the impact they make on other persons

Since they are about to start in a most unfamiliar fashion

each upon their own substantial enquiry, they will soon discover that the facts and opinions they collect in the field, and that therefore determine their progress, depend, more than upon anything else, upon their personal abilities to stimulate those among whom they conduct their enquiries.

3 To equip them with a rudimentary set of ideas useful in their coming set discussions

They will badly need a verbal currency for evaluating their inspirations and for bartering among themselves the advice and criticism constantly surging within their imaginations. Whereas we are not short of a terminology when we are exchanging programmed knowledge, P, we cannot yet be sure of the more economical concepts useful for the mutual definition of Q. However this may be, the following six have been used since the early days of Action Learning, and seem to stand up well:

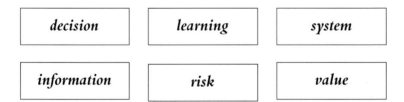

decision	learning	system
information	risk	value

This brief induction course ought to last but a few hectic days. Then, after a short period of field investigation the participants should be re-assembled for a half-day, so that they can let each other, and the course organizers, know of any gaps in their programmed knowledge they already sense may hamper the smooth running of their new enquiries.

PROGRAMME PHASES

The phases of the typical Action Learning programme are described under four headings:

- Diagnosis
- Six sequential phases
- Intermediate invigoration
- Therapeutic.

Diagnosis

In objective 1 of the induction exercises it is suggested that Action Learning should be explained as something different from traditional instruction. In reality, this difference can be made clear only by the practice of Action Learning, and it is helpful throughout any Action Learning programme to refer back to what has so far been done, and to anticipate what is still to come. Nevertheless, it is useful from the outset to encourage the participants to think of what they are doing as a sequence of several phases.

The first (after the preparatory initiatives of sponsors, the nomination of clients, the specification of projects and the choice of participants) is that of diagnosis. Participants must bring themselves, as they identify their first major job (of tracing the course of action they hope will lead to mastering the problem/opportunity put to them), constantly to see their mission in terms of three diagnostic questions:

- "What are we (the firm I am now helping) really trying to do?"
- "What is stopping us from doing it?"
- "What can we do about it?"

It is from these three primary interrogations that the diagnosis of the project will be accomplished, taking the form of a strategic plan. The elaboration of the three questions will take on every conceivable form, from the opening conversations between the participant and their client, through the formation of a provisional strategy based on further conversations and references to more formal records, to the detailed field testing of the provisional strategy among those far from the places of the original conversations.

The avenues likely to be explored by an intelligent outsider cannot possibly be foreseen at the outset, nor can a participant anticipate the unexpected turns the sequence of investigation may take as they report on progress to the other participants in the set.

Six sequential phases

We may summarise the elaboration of an action plan based on these diagnostic questions as the preparation for taking such action. This, it is hoped, will be achieved during the remaining period of the programme, which we call the therapeutic (or action) phase.

In practice, to split the period over which the participant occupies themself with treating the troubles of some other enterprise into two phases in this way is somewhat simplistic. Diagnosis (finding what to do) and therapy (getting it done) rarely fit end to end; they are intermixed to such an extent that a further therapeutic step often demands unravelling much of the previous diagnosis, and making a fresh start. All the same, the sequential notion is important; one ought never to try doing anything important without first finding out what it is being done for.

And if this cautionary approach is looked at in more

detail, we discover that the two phases are each themselves composed of three sub-phases. It is helpful that the participants should discuss these from time to time. In addition to the six ideas forming the vocabulary of debate, these six sequential phases will help them to keep their bearings during the exploration of the previously unknown. The six sequential phases are:

Analysis

From the diagnostic questionings of the previous section, conducted among a wide range of people influential in the affairs of the receiving enterprise, and helped by conversation with the client and discussions within the set, each participant provisionally identifies the key avenues of enquiry to follow.

Development

The participant sets out to find the paper answers to as many of these key questions as they can; this quite specific search will take them to sources of information and opinion whose reliability and political alignment they are soon able to judge, and whose responses may cause them to modify their earlier goals.

Procurement

As the participant begins to see opening up before them a line of enquiry not only suggested in the analysis phase but confirmed in the development, they will start to make provision for exploring it still further, generally by asking whether they can marshal the resources needed to move along it. These may include not only finance or other tangible assets, but also the support of persons throughout the enterprise not involved in the project from the outset.

In some projects it may also be necessary for the

participant to win over some that see this mission as a threat to their own interests.

Construction or assembly

The proposed resources must now be marshalled, so that the individual collaborators and their assets are usefully brought into contact with each other.

At this phase it is likely that there will be a mass return to the first phase, followed by a hurried retracing of steps, since the commitment of resources cuts more deeply than the communication of opinion, and a few fresh questions are likely to be uncovered. At this phase the role of the client becomes of greatest importance, and every effort that the participant has made in the earlier phases to gain their confidence will be abundantly rewarded.

Application

The newly assembled resources in their great variety are set moving in accordance with the original strategy, as this is seen to lie at the end of the provisional avenue of enquiry (suitably modified by the experiences of later phases).

At this phase the participant will be able to identify their true allies, and also the extent of the support from the client and sponsor. It is generally during this application phase (not seldom crowded into the final days of a project whose earlier phases have been allowed to over-run) that fresh key questions are uncovered - and therefore projects defined for future Action Learning programmes.

Review

As the application phase begins to acquire its own momentum and the field work of the project is taken over by the local management, the participant will need to identify to what extent his or her efforts, and those of the local management, have achieved what, from the analysis phase above, they were intended to achieve, and what is to be learned by tracing the major surprises.

It may well be unsophisticated to suggest that, if any Action Learning programme is to run for six months and to pass through these six identifiable (even if overlapping) phases, every participant should spend about one month in each phase.

The real world, full of uncertainty, misrepresentation and doubt, cannot so readily be partitioned. Nevertheless, unsophisticated or not, the sequence is useful in guiding the approach of participants, forcing upon them the planning of their time, and thus giving their whole set a common calendar inside which they may be able to help each other (as the cycle of the seasons may help the farmer) to keep their bearings in what might otherwise degenerate into an unending political dogfight staged in some unmapped industrial wilderness.

The identification of the six sub-phases also helps to discriminate between diagnosis and therapy, since the first three are diagnostic and the latter three therapeutic. The diagnostic phases call only for intellectual skills, providing that the participant is polite, and sufficiently sensitive to the impression they are making upon others not to test too severely the patience of those from whom they are endeavouring to extract suggestions, or merely factual data. The second three phases present an ordeal of a more painful kind, since the participant now seeks from others, not simply an account of what may be going on or an interpretation of its causes and its consequences, but commitment and support. The extent to which he or she secures them will depend upon many things, but mostly, in the early days, upon their personal skills, by which to convince others to a level at which they agree to act in addition to accepting the intellectual argument that action might be quite a good thing to take - provided it is somebody else who takes it.

This is the crucial difference between Action Learning and case studies, authoritarian instruction and all traditional teaching - one has to know not only what is good, but how to do it. Experience of several hundred Action Learning programmes shows that most busy managers follow particular new lines of action, not so much because they are convinced by the logic behind them, but because of their personal belief in the other person advocating to them the innovation. (It is, of course, true, as the history of Action Learning itself reveals, that all fundamental innovation, by whomsoever it is first advocated, is at once ridiculed and then opposed, and all participants must develop the ability to incorporate such rejection into their plans.)

Thus, a well-designed Action Learning programme must engender within each participant the self-confidence that enables them to convince others that their advice is worth following simply because it is the person themselves who offers it. So it is that each participant must find out, in the course of the programme, a lot of things about themselves that they did not know when they joined it. (What is an honest man or woman, and what need I do to become one?)

Intermediate invigoration

The diagnostic phase may prove exhausting, and for strange reasons. Busy managers, many of whom as a matter of settled policy rush off at once to implement the first idea to cross their minds, may find their new role as a participant, first committed to a long search for diagnostic material, more than frustrating.

The perpetual checks and revisions they encounter in discussion with their clients and in argument within their sets are, for some, almost debilitating. Many of them learn to be satisfied, as they tread this arduous course towards the elaboration of their strategy, with little demonstrations of their personal or professional skills made by helping out their field acquaintances, or the local management, with the solution of minor puzzles, or the offering of advice once they are sure that advice will be accepted.

But, over and above these minor restorations of confidence, it is a good thing to offer all the participants a chance, half-way down the programme, to exhibit their findings to an intelligent audience ready and able to respond. In the Belgian programme the participants were taken to USA to argue their findings and suggestions with interested businessmen and celebrated academics (not at that historic period yet suspected of actually harming the economy). This is an experience not easy to replicate in these more austere times, but sets can now present an account of what they have been up to in the first three sub-phases of their endeavours to other sets in the same, or other programmes.

In a large concern, committed to Action Learning for some time ahead, where one set may overlap another in time, that which is half-way through can present its provisional strategy at the end of its diagnostic phase both upstream and down. It can present to the next lot starting out as part of its induction course, trying to identify what, with the benefit of three sub-stages of hindsight, they might have done differently. And it can present to the lot just finishing, in the hope of constructive suggestions about the snags their proposals for action are likely to encounter. Just as participants learn with and from other participants, so may sets (each of which generates a distinctive character of its own) learn with and from other sets just as, in the early 1970s, the participants from Belgium set off to the Nile Project of Egypt and the Egyptian managers came to Brussels to see what the Belgians were doing.

Therapeutic

After their intermediate invigoration, the participants must brace themselves to set out on the most difficult part of the programme: getting firm action to be taken upon what has so far largely been an exercise in intellectual argument and dialectical compromise.

It will be no demanding task to make clear to them the change in the course of their fortunes and responsibilities. But there is one idea that should have been put into their minds long before, and should now be seen as coming into its own: the client group. This is the little band of allies each participant should have been recruiting, under the patronage of their client, as they struggled through the diagnostic phase. The participant should soon be aware that, in this life, very little can be done without allies. Their role is to persuade up to a dozen of those with whom they have been working for the past few months to form, with the client as leader and themselves as convenor and adviser, a team to get implemented the strategy that they have so far helped to draw up.

Three classes of membership are called for:

- Who knows about (understands) the
  problem being tackled?

- Who cares (genuinely wants something done) about the problem?
- Who can (has enough power to) get something useful done about it?

It is now, more than ever, the duty of the participant to observe what goes on in the micro-political arena, where they are acting on behalf of their client. The participant's personal task is to encourage the client group to follow the strategy through under the approval of the client themselves, even if regular meetings of the client group cannot be held. In this uncertain temptation of Providence the participant will do well to bear in mind the findings of Thomas Joh (set out in Chapter 4, below) and she or he will also discover the rewards for their earlier patience in making a personal friend of their client. As one Belgian participant put it: "Always nurse your client; you have no other source of power."

SUPPORTING ASSEMBLIES

The need to hold occasional assemblies of sponsors or of clients as any Action Learning programme unfolds will soon make itself apparent. Save for those organised to get the programme itself started, the participants themselves are the best judges to propose when their seniors might get together and what they might wish to discuss or to suggest.

Sponsors and clients are often known to seek attendance at a set meeting, and for many different reasons, but it should be for the participants to settle on what terms these visitors are admitted. Set meetings are also effective in converting the most determined opponents of Action Learning, the personnel and training staffs to its harmless cause. But it must be remembered that interruptions by outsiders to the deep and very personal involvement of the participants in each others projects will be violently resented, and it is not unknown for behavioural scientists to be physically thrown out of the meeting room when incautious enough to offer professional advice to managers with real tasks to accomplish.

It is in getting participants to report to meetings of others - sponsors, clients, academics, training officers, and so forth - rather than in having them submit to being observed at work that the set procedures will be better understood. So profound may be the impact of self-disclosure upon the individual that any intervention by strangers, even if claiming to be expert in psychology, may be harmful.

The suggestion that the participants themselves, going through these experiences, should keep careful records of what they see happening to them, chronicles of such standards as to conform with those of post-graduate dissertations, has much to commend it. One university is already awarding its masters degrees in this field, and the regular assemblies of the participants who have followed its programmes (run in the closest co-operation with industry and commerce) will eventually have a deep impact upon the development of Action Learning as such and upon the future of higher education as an investment of human resources.

EPILOGUE

This chapter on logistics, although the longest in our compendium, is necessarily most incomplete and sketchy. It makes no effort to discriminate between the logistics of the various exchange options, between full-time and part-time participation, between projects carried out by teams and those by individuals. It says nothing about the role of the supporting staffs, nor about the resolution of conflict, the supplementary studies of participants, the maintenance of a capacity to learn from daily action long after the participant has left the official programme, and many other important considerations.

Most of these omissions are quite deliberate; they have been made to diminish the threat to Action Learning by the professional consultant and the management professor, motivated by personal gain and out to make all in Action Learning as dependent as possible upon the paid expert. This book has been deliberately kept brief, in order that intelligent sponsors, supported by committed clients and motivated participants, will be able to keep themselves clear of the packaged material now flooding the Action Learning market. We need all to learn with and from our comrades in adversity - especially top management. There is no salvation by crackerjacks.

3. The Characteristics of the Manager

IN THIS CHAPTER: The strengths and frailties of those called upon to act as leaders, and the mission of Action Learning to help in their development and correction.

Contents

3 The Characteristics of the Manager

At 70 years of age everyone is a walking expression of the habits of a lifetime and, before that, an emblem of their trade. Few would mistake a ballet dancer for a pugilist, or a miner for a trawler hand, as at first glance one reads the accumulated history of their lives. What, then, are the evidences of being a manager so striking that they must be the foundations on which all management education should rest?

We are considering managers and management in general, seeking out their highest common factors, and cannot discuss here in detail the peculiarities of every class. No doubt, the qualities needed to manage, say, Eddystone lighthouse have little in common with those looked for when appointing the Governor of the Bank of England - whatsoever metaphors may be thought up of rays of hope and darkening nights.

A content analysis of several hundreds of hours of tape-recorded argument between managers in the major Action Learning programmes of Belgium reveals four characteristics, alike in their own spontaneous assertions and in response to others. All may, from time to time, be handicaps no less than assets, and it is their dual character that justifies their choice as the elements of Action Learning. They are:

- the idolisation of past experience, as this is interpreted and recalled
- the charismatic influences of other managers seen as being successful
- the drive towards immediate activity, getting something done now
- the need to keep others in their places.

It is easy to see that all of these are necessarily the marks of the professional manager, the man (or woman) called upon to produce or maintain desired order in any complex system that, sooner or later, will otherwise show signs of falling apart. We may expand a little more upon the four.

IDOLISATION OF PAST EXPERIENCE

Just as all persons embrace within themselves the record of their lives, so are all managers branded by their past experiences; in a profession so dependent upon success, and so punished by failure, every manager has a vivid recollection of triumph and disaster. In consequence, he or she is often unable to see any more in the present than still further confirmation of a past now unforgettable: the misty ghosts of yesterday enshroud what goes on now.

CHARISMATIC INFLUENCES OF OTHERS

Most managers, when in a fix, wonder what So-and-so, the hero whom they have long worshipped, would do; some will reject solutions to current troubles by remarking that, had the proposal any merit, the Duke of Wellington would already have thought of it; some would sooner refer to the biography of the hero than give the same time to looking more closely into the current facts. This may be an ancient and atavistic trait, of which we read even in the Book of Genesis: "There were giants in the earth in those days. . . mighty men which were of old, men of renown." (*Genesis* ch.6 v. 4)

The acceptance of Action Learning in Britain is due to the example of Lord Weinstock trying it out, at first with mixed results, in the most successful company in the country. In its more available forms, charisma will flow from personal contacts with other managers who set their examples of shrewdness and integrity to those around them looking for help.

THE DRIVE TO ACT

Most managers, tormented by the ticking of the office clock and the fall of the days from the factory calendar, will respond sooner to the urgencies of the moment, howsoever inconsequential, than to the suggestion that they ought to clear the decks and heed the long-term warnings. This is the Gresham's law of management: Short-term issues soon drive out the long. Thus one observes the managerial chefs singing as they peel the managerial spuds, or rolling up their sleeves to scour out the administrative pans.

THE NEED FOR ALL TO KNOW THEIR PLACES

In all there is to do, the manager must lead the team, and to conquer its untidy and uncertain world the team must first itself be tidy. From long experience of taking charge and of issuing the instructions for others - this job here, that job there and the other job somewhere else - many managers tend to underrate their staffs. In some enterprises the play of politics may reward this natural touch, so that senior ranks hold totally unrealistic assessments of their relations down below.

BUILDING THE FOUR-SQUARE PROGRAMME

Action Learning programmes should be designed to exploit to the maximum extent these four characteristics of the managerial demand. There will be those who ask why what is already so obvious needs to be set out in such elaboration - or even to be set out at all. Of course, responsibility is searing, and our memories do not forget. Of course, the genius impresses, and we seek him as our model. Of course, we are engaged to get results, and time must not be wasted. Of course, we are in charge, and the rest must look to us. These may be ancient truths, but we can make of them new use, and this is what Action Learning tries to do.

1 The programme must, continuously, emphatically, by responsible conduct and evident trial, oblige each participant to look critically at their past experience, to read afresh the graffiti scrawled across their cortical slate.

Whatever the deliberated activity, whether in a project carried out elsewhere, away from normal work, or whether a study of something supposed to be going on closer home, the participant's next important moves, in diagnosis, prescription or therapy, should be so clearly expounded, so logically justified and so honestly reported back in their outcome, that recollections of the past become the most vivid and steadfast luminance to guide their current strivings, rather than those flickering uncertainties of insight that heighten their perplexities at work.

Since the Action Learning set is inspired by the interest each participant arouses in drawing out the aid of their colleagues towards his or her own success, all will constantly be required to expose for the most exacting scrutiny just what they think they are up to - and why. Yet even at the end of the programme some keen-eyed observer may still be musing over what frightful thing could have happened long ago to a colleague, permanently to obscure from him some glaring weakness of perception. As it was put by one senior Belgian manager: "After three months, they all read my thoughts more clearly than I did myself."

And what one person may take as loyalty to their own past, another sees as treachery to all our futures.

2 Every participant will, from time to time, find themselves down another blind alley, when they will discover for themselves (and be obliged to confess to their colleagues) that there is little point in asking what their charismatic hero would have done.

They will soon be told to get back to the hard realities and forget the sacred shrines. If this person is out of ideas, or needs to face mounting opposition on the job, the colleagues will help them more clearly to perceive where they must look, for in doing so and in discussing why they are doing so they will also be strengthening themselves.

The mind gone blank can do little with itself save panic, but a few supportive minds aware that they themselves might, too, go blank at any moment can provide the most refreshing tonic. It will be that person's own inspiration they will restart, read from that person's own cortex, expressed in that person's own terms and applied in that person's own way; the friends in need are, to be sure, the friends indeed. So, when all else fails, get into Action Learning; by helping others we learn to help ourselves.

3 The longer term study, for which as the co-ordinator of some complex project the participant will now have time enough, enriched by the duty to themselves and to their colleagues to set forth what it all means, not in some instant gabble on the classroom floor led by an impatient teacher, but in the regular calendar of set discussion (when all must explain their confusions no less than their grasps), will also favour the wider vision.

By needing to crawl along its subterranean labyrinths, each participant will come to respect the subtleties and the contradictions that compose their project; all these they will seek to balance and to record, constantly stopping and turning to ask what is still unseen. In this exploration they will put aside instant response and turn to considerate reflection, distinguishing between what is immediately verifiable and what calls for logical analysis leading into testable relationship.

The dialogue between action in the project field and confrontation with colleagues in the set will soon make the case for seeking the long-term view. The participants then learn the virtue of second thoughts about all that may suddenly cross their minds - with second thinking to match the inspiration and the overall design.

4 These analyses and their cross-questionings will oblige each of the participants, and perhaps in unaccustomed ways, to verify their facts more rigorously than in the past.

In a strange environment they may stop to examine, more critically than at home, all that comes to them as information, by what channels it does so, and what, if any, uses are now made of it by those at lower levels.

The participant's status in the receiving enterprise, together with their own personal desire to get at the truth by methods to which they have long been a stranger, will suddenly make them understand how dependent they are - and must necessarily be - upon staff of whose very existence, even upon the organization chart (should one exist), they were formerly quite unaware.

The quest for reliable information upon which to rest one's case when at work away from home is invariably such as to force - although there is much willingness - every participant in an Action Learning programme to rethink what they owe their staff and to re-examine their own credentials to be their leader. It was the controller of energy at the largest steel plant in Belgium who, as a participant working on the management information system of a savings bank, observed: "It is always the boss who decides whether his staff work well or badly, and power is not always where it seems to be."

A MODEL FOR LEARNING TO ACT

We can easily represent these four elements as the inputs to a model of Action Learning. Each must generate its corresponding output, and encourage the outputs of the other three.

1 Idolisation of the meaning of past experience must be transformed into the constant reappraisal of one's true beliefs and inner resources.

"There is a difference between believing in nothing, on the one hand, and not knowing in what to believe, on the other. I recognise now that I have not only been doing entirely the wrong things in my own job; our salary system was designed for me to concentrate on doing them."

2 The charismatic influences of others, diminishing the ability to seek self-reliance, must open the windows of self-disclosure to admit the friendliness of other learners.

"At first I felt uneasy about my freedom to speak the truth. Why should anybody in my firm be interested in the truth? Now I see no harm in it. Indeed, I occasionally find it quite satisfying. Managers are not untruthful by nature; they are simply forced to pretend that they know even when they do not know."

3 The drive to act must be replaced by a desire to seek out some rational base for operational decisions.

"This programme has taught me always to consider what I should do next. Previously it had never occurred to me to ask. Getting at the real problem is like skinning an onion: the longer it goes on the more people who shed tears."

4 The need for all to know their places must become an interest in participative leadership, with learning to do the task by the unavoidable need to do it.

"At the start I was convinced that change of any kind was impossible; now I see that, using patience, I have made it inevitable. It is no longer disturbing for me to accept support form another manager without having to negotiate some deal with them."

★

All of these transformations can be helped by the academic syllabus judiciously brought to bear, in forms to be agreed by the participants, preferably after the demand for its help has been made in terms of specific operational need. A dual support is still to be preferred.

In the first element, to relieve a fixation upon the past, the psychology of perception and of defensiveness should be seen against the background of confrontation with other participants about understanding and influencing some accessible reality.

In the second and the fourth elements, each raising dependence on the self and the staff, the conflicts within the set should be discussed in terms of the psychology of the interpersonal, and of such concepts as authority, security and value.

In the third element, with its tantalising and protracted searches of the complex and unfamiliar, we must, if help is sought, call in the business analysts and the modellers of operational research.

SUMMARY

The essential working arrangements of Action Learning provide precisely the developmental needs called for by these four managerial characteristics. Instead of ...

1 ...their long-acquired inclination to see their past successes and their past failures writ large in what they now encounter as the present.

This may be corrected by their constantly having to explain to other attentive managers what they are now engaged upon, what they intend to do about it, and, in particular, how their perception of what they see and their design of what they plan are coloured by their past experiences.

2 ...the identification of their own success with that of some hero-figure (or of more than one), striving to imitate some model rather than to develop their own plans of action from scratch.

By questioning them on how their plans have been drawn up and implemented, their set colleagues force them to make use of their own latent powers. The Prize Song of Wagner's *Die Meistersinger* is an allegory, with Walther, the knight, being cross-questioned by

Hans Sachs, the shoemaker, as to how he had first been inspired to compose his imperfect draft.

3 ...their preoccupation with short term issues in the hope of quick rewards, rather than with the longer term issues more important to the future (a misdirection of attention said to have been a cause of industrial troubles in the USA).

An Action Learning project, by its very nature, forces every participant to examine the roots of strategy, and also denies access to short-run trials.

4 ... their unrealistic views of the supporting roles of their staff, leading to exaggerated estimates of their own powers of leadership.

Action Learning exercises conducted away from home soon force participants to acknowledge their dependence upon those at lower levels - especially for the facts about what may be going on, as distinct from what is thought to be going on.

The participants will soon become aware of these four characteristics and of the ways in which they are illuminated by the programme. They may go so far as to ask that supplementary courses, over and above the field exercises, should be arranged for the deeper analysis of the psychological and technical issues raised in the identification of these four characteristics.

This implies, of course, that the programme will now start to provide P. Since what is now specifically asked for is highly relevant to the needs of the participants it will stimulate, rather than retard, their total learning. As far as possible, P should be supplied by other participants when it falls in the fields of professional managers - as in accountancy, quantitative methods, systems design, capital investment, warehousing and distribution, wages policy and so forth. Not all participants, of course, will have the same needs, and all supplementary enlightenment of this nature should be individually specified.

4. The Influence of Top Management

IN THIS CHAPTER: An analysis of the responses of top managements to their own efforts to improve what was going on in their own enterprises.

Contents

* NOTE: A doctoral research project carried out in the University of Brussels by a candidate from South Korea, Thomas Joh (but in no way associated with the design or running of the inter-university programme and attached to a department similarly uninvolved), has supplied the Action Learning literature with a system of classification of the twelve attitudes of top management towards this approach to the problems of industry and commerce. A brief account of the conclusions of this singular study is given here, not because it suggests how the influences of these key persons may be securely recruited in support of Action Learning, for of these recondite affairs we know very little. It is offered here as something to alert those embarking on the logistical uncertainties of setting up a real programme, among real people, to tackle challenges in real time.

4 The Influence of Top Management*

"As the judge of the people is himself, so are his officers; and whatsoever a man the ruler of the city is, so are all they who inhabit therein."(Ecclesiasticus ch.x v.2)

If, as the writer of Ecclesiasticus (and a hundred of his imitators) will persist in telling us, it is the attitude of the boss that counts most in the end, then, if we cannot change that attitude after the programme has begun, let us at least ask ourselves how much we can detect of it before we set out. All this chapter has to say is about the influence of different attitudes of top management. It leaves it to the organisers of possible programmes to detect what these might be.

CARTE BLANCHE CONFIDENCE

Top management, right from the start, shows complete confidence in all aspects of the programme, from their response to the original invitation to take part in it to their willingness for personal association with the field work and its reaction back on the daily operations of their enterprise.

They are, at the outset, anxious to define their own roles, notably by giving thought to the selection of the problem/opportunity to be worked on, by making known throughout the management that they are personally involved in the study, and, above all, by being reasonably available to those at lower levels trying to achieve what the project is being shaped to achieve. They are aware that the participant comes to them as a learner, not an expert adviser, and that the experience they are now to undergo as a learner in a strange environment will engender learning among others, as among themselves. They do not conceal from the participant their understanding that this mission is unusual, and are reasonably willing to discuss its unexpected turns.

ACTIVE CO-OPERATION

Top management is open and receptive, but without actively recognising that they, too, are bound to be important learners within the system, if it is to be as successful in its mission as expected.

Apart from this they are ready to go out of their way to ensure that all the other conditions needful for the success of the project are fulfilled – including the goodwill and support of senior managers and heads of departments.

ENCOURAGING ATTENTIVENESS

Top management displays a paternal interest, but is careful not to give the impression of taking any significant initiative.

They show from their meetings with the participant, invariably called at that person's request, that they have grasped what is going on and remain ready to give whatsoever support is still needed. But they are not forthcoming and the participant gains no sense that these meetings, although businesslike and helpful to advancing the project, leave them with any belief that the top managers themselves are contributing much to a task that the majority within the enterprise would consider badly in need of doing.

CIRCUMSPECT ALLIANCE

While continuing their support for any measures that may need their formal agreement (such as extending enquiries into affiliated organizations, or out among customers), top management gives the unmistakable impression of not wanting to be associated with any direction the project may be assuming.

They take no initiatives on leads offered by the participant, nor do they suggest fresh interpretations of what may be emerging from the study.

NON-HOSTILE SCEPTICISM

Top management is unwilling to take risks or open up new avenues of enquiry unless the participant can produce concrete evidence that they will succeed.

They are habitually neutral towards the project, except when they might agree to apply its findings to amend an occasional paragraph in the works code.

Lack of interest

Top management gives the participant no particular attention, and they may have difficulty even in making appointments with the client.

The participant may ask for what reason the receiving enterprise entered the programme in the first place. Nevertheless, the encouragement and support of colleagues in the set help to maintain the interest of the participant, since the pathological condition of the host management is a constant challenge to these others, providing them with a background for getting into perspective some of their own obstructions.

Such, indeed, is the cohesion of the sets brought about by the comradeship in adversity of the participants that, even with lack of interest so remarkable that the mere continuance of the enterprise is a source of astonishment, no participant has yet withdrawn; apparently the chance of observing at close hand the featureless routines of a profitable mediocrity can prepare a vigorous observer to scale the summits of imagination on returning to their own command at the end of the programme.

Manipulative guidance

Top management seeks to run the project without giving the game away to such an extent that they lose the goodwill and co-operation of their participant.

The top management seem to have some pretty-well-thought-out remedial plan of their own, which might have to face a rough reception were it applied other than through the agency of a programme that their subordinate managers might one day wish to apply for. For a self-assured participant with the backing of their colleagues such a top management offers the best of all challenges. They are out to get something done, have reasonably sound, if preconceived ideas, and desire to keep the personal friendship of their participant, although they may not want to listen attentively to their early suggestions.

TACTICAL PROCRASTINATION

Top management seeks continually to gain time; whatever detail each turn of the project brings forth is examined under the most elaborate argument.

They seem motivated by either or both of the following:

- The fear that any strategic (non-departmental) action will disturb some existing truce between those in command of such departments; or
- The hope that the project will one day come upon, perhaps by contrived accident, some compromise solution acceptable to all.

Thus, until the day when the participant suddenly gets warm, they must be headed off any course of action likely to demand significant shifts of senior status.

Diagnostic inflexibility

Top management refuses to consider the suggestion that the initial formulation of the problem/opportunity around which the project is supposed to be designed was misconceived.

This is very frequently so, and the question chosen to be answered often turns out to be one of several, or subsidiary to a question more expressive of the need for top management to change their policies. In many instances, therefore, it is apparent early on in the programme that little is likely to be gained by confining the project to the limits first drawn around it. Nevertheless, a few top managements still look to their participant to provide them with an expert solution to a minor difficulty, and to leave its deeper causes untreated.

Evasion and vacillation

Top management systematically shears away from the discussion of thorny issues, hesitates even to explore any topic that may be contentious, and is particularly anxious to avoid the suggestion that its troubles may be organic.

Their attitudes are similar to those in the category above, save that they are ready to agree that the first formulation of the project theme may be replaced by something wider. But, whereas those above are ready to see action taken upon an unimportant issue – and a limited action, at that – those in this category seem unable to face action of any kind.

DIRECTIVE AUTOCRACY

Top management is very clear and very efficient on a misinterpretation of the exercise.

They see their participant as a skilled executive lent to them to implement their own unilateral plans. They refuse to entertain fresh major ideas emerging from the study, and may even go so far as to ask that all correspondence with the participant is conducted in writing.

DEFENSIVE RATIONALISATION

Top management seeks to explain away, by whatever argument may be at hand, every element in the ideas put forward by the participant, including the facts on which those elements are drawn, to suggest the nature (even, at times, the very existence) of any problem/opportunity.

This is not because, as some participants in the set of their colleague faced with these attitudes have suggested, the top management is amplifying their own learning by playing the devil's advocate. Like others above, they seem unwilling to ask whether their problems may not be deeper than suspected.

The inconsistencies of their objections are a considerable challenge to the participant, who needs to direct the attention of the board to the possibility that their true difficulties lie in conflict between themselves. In one celebrated instance, the participant who had pointed this out to his hosts without effect at the time, was called back nearly two years later, when their internal stresses had reached so high a level that they were ready to discuss them with one who already had their confidence.

★

Some of these responses of top management may seem surprising when first encountered. But they are all illustrations of propositions in social psychology identified long ago. Many persons read in messages only what they wish to read; others persistently refuse to listen to bad news of any kind, although the practice of shooting the messenger conveying it has long fallen into disuse. Political in-fighters rarely wish to be disturbed by suggestions concerning long range truth; those poised in some delicate balance of administrative or political power have their own ways of filtering reports that might lead to some fresh equilibrium.

The idolisation of the past provides its own framework for classifying more recent impressions. Evidence that such-and-such is amiss may be too trivial to engage any attention, but if it is added to, and the trouble seems to get worse, then this may goad the system to act – until still more bad news takes things beyond the limits of correction, and the system pretends that, since nothing can be done, no further messages are called for. Those who would cheerfully tackle one deficiency, on hearing that their task is to look into something else altogether, will often withdraw their attention completely, so that nothing at all is done.

All of these principles of human fallibility are clearly shown in these programmes, and those who set out to design still more should do what they can to prepare the top management to accept the role so critical to the success of the venture.

THE EFFECT OF TOP MANAGEMENT ATTITUDE

Dr Joh [referred to in the Note at the beginning of this chapter] was able to categorise the outcomes of 35 completed assignments in which the visiting participants were all able to spend their full term of nine months working solely in their host enterprises, undisturbed by mergers, departmental reorganization or other vital influence, such as a major promotion for the participant even when away from his own enterprise. Dr Joh identified four orders of outcome:

- Concrete application of recommendations flowing from project.

- Acceptance of recommendations for future application.

- Resistance to changes sufficient to prolong study beyond period foreseen.

- Cases defying analysis through insufficient evidence of outcome.

These may be related to the 12 top management attitudes set out above. With 12 times 4, or 48, cells for classification and 35 outcomes to classify our task must be simplified. Thus we collapse the 12 classes of top management attitude into positive, or knowingly helpful, and negative, or not overtly encouraging; likewise, the four classes of outcome are collapsed into two, successful and negative/neutral. The two-by-two Contingency Table in Fig. 2 shown on p.70, is with an association between attitudes and outcome significant at less than one per cent.

Fig 2.   Contingency Table

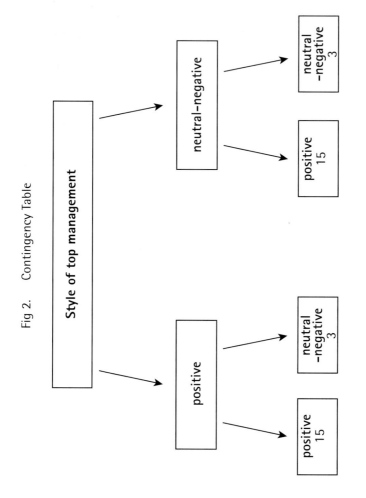

Chi-square (Yates' correction) 8.295: significance P=0.4%

5. The Philosophy of Action Learning

IN THIS CHAPTER: A short development of the ancient thesis that there can be no learning without action and no action without learning.

Contents

5 The Philosophy of Action Learning

REFLECTION AND ACTION: LEARNING BY DOING

It is many years since Aristotelianism was first recognised as a way of looking at the world, by those who insisted that experimental verification was a more reliable guide to mastering what they felt called upon to do than was intuitional plausibility. Finding out if something works when we try it still promises us more percentage than does checking it from a book or arguing about it with somebody else.

Aristotle, too, has bequeathed to us a system of ethics balanced upon action and reflection; one gets to understand by doing, and to do by understanding. Thus it is that Aristotle is another of the Patriarchs to whom the opponents of Action Learning may be referred – along with Buddha, Sophocles and St James. Only in recent times, with the rise of book learning, 'credentialism', tenured jobs at universities, professional institutions granting permission to add letters after one's name, and so forth, has education started marketing the pretence that to know and to do are quite unrelated expressions of the human spirit, as opposed as Heaven and Earth, as categorically distinct as soul and body, as different as day and night.

Action Learning is the Aristotelian manifestation of all managers' jobs: they learn as they manage, and they manage because they have learned – and go on learning. As an activity in its own right, namely, something about which books have been written, courses organized, packages of every kind sold on the commercial market, Action Learning has been obliged to evolve simply to protect real managers from the corruption of a lucrative academicism, enticing honest and responsible subjects to kid themselves that they will more effectively fulfil their missions by listening to lectures, by reading books and by being led through the simulations of unreal or idealised experience.

In the light of unsophisticated Nature there would be no need for Action Learning, since there would arise no artificial management education demanding to be opposed by it. Those who plied responsible trades would artlessly exchange accounts of what they got done, and ask each other all about what they had failed to get done, unhindered by professional interceptors, commentators, analysts, consultants, interpreters, reviewers and other experts.

It is to counteract what these obscurantist supernumeraries are up to that Action Learning has been obliged to distil a literature from its own hard-won experience, but its pages are no more than a guide to encourage others to make a start upon learning from reality. The day that Action Learning is said to be enshrined within its own encyclopaedia will be the day to read out its obituary. And, until then, we must also remember that Aristotle did not always follow his own precepts and check his theories; his teaching that bodies fall faster when heavier survived until Galileo – nearly 2,000 years.

Managers as 'Action Reflectors' or as 'Learner Doers'

By doing what they set out to do, and by setting out to do what they believe to be worth doing, managers are disciples of the Aristotelian ethic.

After reports about all the facts have reached their desks, after all the advice has been offered, all the opinions listened to, after everything has been listed for the final plan and the most talkative of the experts is on their way back to the airport deciding in advance what they are going to tell the next client, the manager still remains alone with the responsibilities: he or she is the person who has to get something done. Specialists have uttered their warnings, research consultants have thrown doubt upon the accuracy of the data, local academics have drawn attention to the precedent of The Taff Vale judgment, the public relations officer sees certain weaknesses if the affair has to be reported on the international network, and the economic adviser, while voicing no views about the cash flow, still shakes his head, knits his brow and purses his lips about the cash flow situation. But the manager alone has to do something about it all .

The importance of action and lived experience

One mission of Action Learning is to help the manager bear this special burden. Educational programmes that fall short of this, that do not prepare for this critical role by extending into it, are actually designed to emphasise the fallacy that talking about taking action is no different from engaging in the action being talked about … and thus that those who talk about it deserve to be paid at the same rate as those who finally take it. Their argument gains plausibility because the antecedents of responsible action can be so richly set forth in words and figures that these symbols, marshalled in their imposing administrative ceremonials, may divert attention from what needs now to be done, reducing it to the squalid lumberings of a handful of men in bowler hats.

These sophistries would not impress the characters in *The Cherry Orchard*, holding forth at length upon how they have talked themselves out of all capacity to act. We know today, a full lifetime after Chekov, that the business school graduates regarded by their professors as the most brilliant of their case analysis, and still rising like meteors in their first jobs, are overhauled and passed by middle life. Those who seemed less able, back in the seminar room, to keep afloat in the monsoons of dialectic, remained free until their maturity to discover for themselves the powerful truths of their own lived experience.

Unlike their sparkling classmates, trained to turn on at will their fountains of purest rhetoric uncontaminated by passing doubt, they could not set aside what they had learned of the world at first hand, and so were delayed along the way by the shifting cargo of the experiences they had taken aboard. It demanded of them another decade to learn how these accumulations should be most economically stowed and most profitably traded; it was no longer sufficient, as in the days of the seminar, that the containers should be empty and the voyage chalked across a blackboard. Life, as Aristotle still reminds some of us, is made up of action as well as of reflection.

Knowing means doing

We demand that each participant attacks a real-life task for which no course of treatment has yet been suggested, even although efforts have already been made to do so. The problem may or may not be in the organization by which the participant is, at the time, employed, nor need it be in any professional field of their acquaintance. The programme is to help the manager develop as a manager, not as a business consultant, a staff adviser, a specialist in such-and-such a field or an expert in some other.

She or he is there to observe themselves in managerial action, trying to produce desired order in some totality judged to be in need of it, to effect some specified change in a complexity alike ill-structured and inconstant, to make helpful allies of some whose interests are at risk, of others who would undermine their authority, and of many who hold certificates proving that they understand the theory of the firm.

It is thus essential that the client management who own and offer the problem or opportunity which the participant is to tackle are genuinely motivated to tackle it, and have made this clear to the staff with whom the visitor is to work. Many Action Learning exercises are less effective than they might be on account of shyness among those who carry such final responsibilities; there is even a little evidence that the popular image of those at the top struggling, like Prometheus and Laocoon, against overwhelming odds, is not invariably appropriate.

And moreover, if the clients are merely seeking some analysis of their difficulty, howsoever elaborate and sophisticated, charged with whatsoever recommendations, they must not be encouraged to think that they are into Action Learning. Managers are not employed to describe, to analyse or to recommend. They are engaged to act. This they start to achieve more effectively only after they are able to see the outcomes of their own deliberated plans, implemented by themselves rather than by others who had no hand in their preparation or no faith in their validity.

The primacy of the set

In the risk-laden predicament of innovation each manager needs the support, not of those expert in yesterday's successes, but of their fellow managers going through the same tricky apprenticeship of facing tomorrow's confusion. To provide this support, and to encourage their sagacity still more by offering the same support back to their fellows, is another aim of Action Learning. The primary market for these exchanges is the small and stable set of comrades in adversity, regularly disciplining themselves in their observations and their analyses, more realistically appraising and more sensitively applying the limitless stores of their own lived experience.

All the paraphernalia described here (of clients and client groups, models of diagnosis and therapy, the sequential order of successful achievement, the climatology of top management, the occupational traits of managers themselves as human beings, the guile of micro-politics and so forth) – all as moulded in the Action Learning experiments of the past thirty years – have been isolated and defined merely to reinforce the character of the set as the mirror in which the real-life action is reflected, not only from one participant to the next, just as are the empty containers pushed around the case discussion, but also between the mind of the participant and the real world to which they will shortly return with their container freshly charged.

We must be wary, now that Action Learning seems to

gain acceptance, that the set is not cut off from reality, sold as a part-time discussion group of four or five top managers meeting to exchange their unverified misconceptions as to what may be going on under their command.

PROJECTS FOR ACTION; SETS FOR REFLECTION

It may well be the set that most forcibly expresses the Aristotelian idea of which Action Learning is a modern example.

The set has been deliberately contrived so that managerial reflection can play upon the action of yesterday and anticipate the action of tomorrow. It reminds its members that when tomorrow arrives, with its call for them to do something, that very doing must itself remember not only yesterday's reflection, but that reflection as it must be modified by the here-and-now dispositions of the moment making up the present – dispositions that could have been but imperfectly imagined during yesterday's set exchanges.

Action Learning not only exalts Aristotelianism by forcing participants to interpret all they are doing through the looking glasses of reflective argument; it obliges them constantly to polish the glasses so as to ensure its images are clearly seen. Whether each participant wipes clean their own mirror, or whether this is done for them by another member of the set, cannot be foretold. All the same, it would be wrong to assume that the spirit of Aristotle informs only the set itself; there are other components of Action Learning programmes to prove that doing is knowing and that knowing is doing. Together they compose our educational task force, although the set may be the flag-ship that most boldly carries the Aristotelian banner.

The learning community

This force, which we may call the learning community, must include the senior management deciding from the outset to be in the programme, and, as is clear from other references in this monograph, critically influential in determining how much is learned and how much progress is made. And each participant will shape the views and draw out the experiences of all with whom they work, infusing at the levels of operation, away from the set, the Aristotelian interplay of action and reflection.

In some of the missions run by the Hospital's Internal Communication Project (HIC) (see Bibliography, below) up to five hundred members of the staff were inspired by their own diagnostic and therapeutic endeavours. It would have been impossible for some antique and stiff-jointed institution like a large London hospital to lift its annual efficiency by the order of a million pounds unless the learning virus injected into a few of the senior staff had diffused down to the bedside and into the laundry. And, no less, it was at these humbler levels that the suggestions about what to do were drawn from what those who worked at them had already done, after these lived experiences, also interpreted in the local mirrors of custom and practice, had been accepted as learning experiences the next time round.

In the first strategic Belgian exchanges (The inter-university programme of 1968; see Bibliography, below) it was estimated that the 21 bartered participants, the substantive set members, strongly influenced over two hundred senior managers in the enterprises that participated. More recent examples show that when Action Learning is accepted as the best means of averting total calamity – as in saving the whole enterprise from collapse – or of securing the highest of rewards – as in winning some contract open to the world – every single member of the management, not merely the nominated members of the set central to the exercise, has been brought to understand the message of Aristotle: that it is from action alone that one learns to act more effectively – using the job as the syllabus and the colleague as the teacher.

OUTWARDS FROM SET TO LEARNING COMMUNITY

Nor are these numerical multipliers the only virtues of the learning community. Each participant influences every other to some observable extent, so that the ideas and experiences of many very different individuals are reflected into another enterprises and into other industries.

One set may learn from another set, as, for example, when the score of participants in a five set programme decide, every five weeks, to regroup themselves for half a session. This is not so as to go into detail through the reflective exercises to which they have accustomed themselves with their regular colleagues, but to analyse with comparative strangers the nature of these exercises rather than their project content. They are getting together to discuss, not so much what can be seen reflected in their individual looking glasses, but how the glasses are most effectively used.

In these exchanges, there is nothing more important than that each should recognise the conditions of their own learning, or what it is that leads them to change their mind, whether from the action they are constrained to take, the new interpretation forced upon them by the comments of a colleague, or by a new skill in holding their own looking glass in a new fashion. It is the social character of all learning (demonstrating A gets nothing from the arguments of B unless B also gets something from the responses of A) that makes it worthwhile for those embarked on Action Learning to concentrate from time to time upon the precise origins of their new insights, and by what means these can then be passed to others.

Aristotle's thesis, that if we are all involved in the action – five hundred of us on the floor of the hospital – then we are also all involved in the learning, offers us, to be sure, our philosophical rewards. Nevertheless, as practical managers, it is good to know in some operational detail how to speed the transmission of the thesis through to those corners of the enterprise as unknown to the members of the set as are those members unknown to those who work in the corners.

Just as sets may resonate with other sets, so also may one organization learn with and from another. Despite Belgium's extreme sensitivity to the state of world commerce (for that country must export half of its gross domestic product to pay for necessities – compared with Britain at less than one quarter, Japan less than one sixth and the US less than one twelfth) Belgium alone in the West kept GDP-per-worker as high in the 1970s as in the 1950s, when even Germany and Japan lost about 3 per cent annually across the tinselled 1960s. But Belgium saw, and in the face of all adversity, how more effectively to use its economic resources, year after year since its strategic programme of top level exchanges was begun.

This quite singular performance supports the Action Learning thesis: that it is adversity which most readily improves our actions, by first concentrating our thoughts, and that the Belgian programme, by starting with the second, has now achieved the first. And if enterprise may learn from enterprise, why not one country from another? Perhaps the more fruitful applications of Action Learning lie, however, in quite other fields – in its promise for industrial democracy, to bring the trade unions and the shop floor into raising the quality of life all round, not in productivity alone. The ills of society, too, in violence, urban decay, unemployment, offer Aristotle their challenges.

THE PRIME IDEA OF ACTION LEARNING

The prime idea of Action Learning, set forth at the end of Chapter 1, is that all rational behaviour, intended by sober deliberation to increase one's command over the environment (with the terms command and environment also soberly deliberated) is that learning, advising and deciding (followed by the action defined by that decision) are inextricably related.

They are, all three, different aspects of the same entity, namely, the sober and deliberated examination of the world around us, made with a view to deepening our understanding of that world – something generally known as scientific research. Although this, like learning, advising and deciding, must also be conducted by human beings, it is a comparatively recent development, and was unknown to many of the civilisations that preceded what we are pleased to call our own. It follows from this prime idea that:

> *There can be no learning without action, and no (sober and deliberate) action without learning.*

There are, of course, many who go on doing the same ineffectual things all their life, and at the end of it they attract the comment, 'There's no fool like an old fool'. But there are also those who soberly and deliberately refuse to learn, because the new knowledge, while consonant with the scientific method, is inconvenient for other reasons. It may not be complying to know such-and-such, just in case it might slip out, or even affect one's actions. It might even be that some new way of looking at how one earns a living lights up a new question: Is my time really well spent?

The truth, should it come, may be painful, and disincline one from taking aboard new beliefs. New ideas suggesting new behaviours may be soberly and deliberately suppressed because they contradict established values and accepted traditions. Thus it was that Nietzsche evaluated any new proposal by the animosity with which it was first received; unless it is ridiculed by the clever and opposed by the stupid, it is not worth going ahead with, for it is only after such rough receptions that it will be absorbed. Certainly, this has been the experience of Action Learning, ridiculed through the 1960s and 1970s by the management schools, but now advertised by them under different names as their own developments.

The criterion by which such behaviour should be judged is not intellectual ability but personal values. The opposition to novelty is not due to pure obtuseness, to an incapacity in following the cycle of the scientific method as it unrolls the truth. It is that the truth contradicts existing values, if these are known; or that it demands facing unpleasant risks if one is to work out the consequences of embracing some different notion.

Thus it was that the single idea discovered by the top

managers in the first inter-university programme of Belgium to be of the greatest interest to them was that of a value system. What were the standards of integrity against which all final judgments were made by those with whom they worked – including themselves? It was a notion bound to arise out of the set discussions in which the participants stripped each other naked, an experience that led them to define the most valuable question they had learned as, "What is an honest man, and what need I do to become one?"

THE PRINCIPLE OF INSUFFICIENT MANDATE

Those to whom this question rarely occurs are unlikely to know who they may be, nor in what they may believe. This means that they have incomplete views of the significance of fresh experience and are, on that account, unlikely to gain much from it. The top Belgian programme was important simply because it greatly enhanced the self-awareness of the participants, teaching them a great deal more about themselves than about management techniques. It was this that led one participant to admit that the set made him feel like a Henry Moore statue, with a great hole in it, through which the other members launched their paper darts at each other. Certainly, it was those who became most aware of themselves who also became most aware of others, and so of their micro-political problems.

All this, inherent in the prime idea of Action Learning, is expressed in The Principle of Insufficient Mandate:

> *Those unable to change themselves cannot change what goes on around them.*

Those who are to change significantly that which they freshly encounter must themselves be changed by the changing of it. Without power to discard beliefs shown to be wrong (insufficient mandate over oneself) one cannot introduce actions known to be right. It is an essential derivative of Action Learning.

6. What Action Learning is Not

IN THIS CHAPTER: An effort to pass the ideas of others off as my own by discriminating between Action Learning and traditional methods.

Contents

6 What Action Learning is Not

We have so far tried to define what Action Learning is supposed to be, mainly by listing the elements of which one will become aware on getting involved in it – as well as by presenting the prime idea as the Figure at end of Chapter 1. But any reference to these elements – characteristic assumptions of Action Learning; essential logistics; characteristics of the manager; influences of top management; philosophy of Action Learning – has generally been met by those coming across Action Learning as a topic of conversation, who themselves have not yet seen it in reality, with a spontaneous rejection, generally expressed in a torrent of academic analogy, "Action Learning? You mean learning by doing? What's new about that? We've got it all; what's more, we've had it all for donkey's years! There's nothing new for us in learning by doing!"

And there will follow much supporting argument from the headings below. These have been prepared to show what Action Learning may be confused with, no doubt, but what, nevertheless, is not Action Learning. All this, and a lot more, about an idea first put forward in 1945.

JOB ROTATION

In this, as it has been explained to me, the learning vehicles are a series of functional tasks, each tried under the tutelage of the person normally in charge of the unit in which those functions are regularly discharged. This overseer (manager, supervisor, specialist, head of department) agrees to induct the novice into the local mysteries, generally with the understanding that they are a temporary visitor, a bird of passage who has just finished a similar sojourn in some other specialist unit and who will move over to another after getting a brief acquaintance of what goes on at this particular spot.

"Sitting next to Nelly" (followed by Kate, Agatha and the rest), or "Getting the Cooks Tour" are variants sometimes used in place of the more official title of job rotation. Where the tradition is tenaciously held that, should two things seem to look alike, they must be identical in all conceivable respects – the principle behind the case method – it follows that Action Learning is, and must necessarily be, equated with job rotation.

In practice, the exchanges within an Action Learning programme are contrived so that the visitor may begin to change the local goings-on, not to rehearse them for implanting elsewhere. If they sit next to Nelly, it is to evaluate what Nelly is up to and to help her do it differently by encouraging her to ask herself and her pals what they are achieving.

Traditionally, one sits next to Nelly for exactly the same purpose as that behind all programmed instruction: to become proficient in yesterday's business, and to convince those who show one how to do so, namely, the Nellies beside whom one sits – or the experts on programmed instruction – that they know better than any others in the world what life is all about. This is, most emphatically, not Action Learning.

PROJECT WORK

As I understand it, this is generally the mission of some working party set up by the top management of an organization to make recommendations (or even to take circumscribed action) about some embarrassment that can no longer be ignored.

Generally, the source of difficulty is already clearly identified by several powerful factions within the organization – although there is also the drawback that each faction sees that source within some department other than its own. Usually the leader of the working party can be anticipated, long before that working party is at last constituted; he is generally the functional expert whose unswerving dedication to the practices of his youth is the fundamental cause of the embarrassment that has now become unendurable.

The status of the members of the project team will also be predictable, although its membership may change from time to time. This will represent the various factions (operating departments, functional advisers, headquarters and regional directors, and so forth), but will not be empowered to contribute anything of moment to the deliberations of the working party without first getting authority from its principals.

A typical working party is, in short, merely a concentrated expression of the very divisiveness that is leading to the collapse of industrial and commercial corporatism. While its counter marching may do much to bring out the rivalries and the contradictions within the body it is supposed to represent, it is no more effective in doing this than has become the British House of Commons; a political coconut-shy for the amusement of a population with more and more time on its hands.

Action Learning has nothing in common with such diversions, but is concerned with encouraging real persons to tackle real problems in real time.

CASE STUDIES, BUSINESS GAMES, OTHER SIMULATIONS

These are normally based on narrow edited descriptions by anonymous writers of unknowable conditions. Evidently the students (participants, discussants, players) can be responsible neither for diagnosis nor for therapy.

The minor disagreements likely to break out among a dozen literate persons reading a document of fifty pages will soon encourage them to take up and defend a dozen different interpretations of what the total document was given to them for. This will soon enable the "case leader" to join in their arguments with all manner of references that, left on their own, the dozen participants could scarcely dream of. Some case leaders are so good at such intervention that they are known in American business schools as "star faculty".

However this may be, the students have no means of checking the stories they are given to read, neither at the level of the facts they are supposed to offer (such as whether the Detroit Transport Corporation actually exists, if it really does have the assets it is said to have, and so forth), nor at the level of the presentation of those facts by the order and emphasis with which they appear (since most persons are willing to agree that a horse chestnut frequently conveys an impression unlike that of a chestnut horse).

In Action Learning, the narrative on which the set discussions are based is dragged slowly and painfully from the here-and-now of the reality that the participant has been invited to diagnose and to treat. She or he themself becomes part of it, and it becomes influenced by their concern for it.

Whereas in the case discussion one particular student may triumph over all their rivals by the sheer loquacity and dialectic with which they marshal the ambiguities and exclusions of the script – and thereby be persuaded that they have in some way triumphed over Managerial Nature Itself – the participant in any Action Learning exercise would know perfectly well that, unless they had themselves marshalled the evidence (by a long and tortuous inquisition as distinct from a glance down some printed page); argued it with a score of others all themselves seeking factual relevance in their own shifting confusions (as distinct from telling a dozen others to read again what it says on page number so-and-so of the case documents); and then tried to get something done about it back in the inferno of reality (as distinct from handing over the papers for the next lot to argue about tomorrow), true learning, that which improves one's command of the adjacent world, is not so easy.

Nor is the simulation made any more real by appealing to the superior organising power of the computer: unreality is not made more substantial by multiplying it a thousand times a second. None of this is Action Learning.

GROUP DYNAMICS AND OTHER TASK-FREE EXERCISES

During the 1960s these exercises proliferated to such an extent that it is risky to assert that none of them contain the essential element of Action Learning – verification in the face of reality rather than by reference to (supposed) principle or to the opinion of other persons.

Indeed, in very recent years, there is now the chance that what had been developed as Action Learning, a consortium of top managers regularly meeting to discuss among themselves the effect of trying out their interpretations of reality back upon the reality itself, may now revert to mere group discussion unverified by subsequent real world comparison. To be sure, it is their own personal perceptions of their own responsible tasks that the handful of participants are on about, and there can be little denying that, in being forced to describe to others what it is they imagine they are up to, their views of what this may be may frequently be modified.

But, if their new perceptions are not soon checked against the real world they purport to reflect – and, preferably, by some test that challenges the responsibility of the manager undertaking to conduct it – none can be sure that the discussions have not so much modified perception in the direction of truthfulness as merely swapped one misunderstanding for another.

There is all the difference in the world between modifying reality, on the one hand, and talking about modifying reality, on the other, even if, in an academic culture based upon talking about what might be done rather than upon the real time doing of it, this difference may frequently escape our attention. Thus it is that, while group dynamics, aimed at trying to demonstrate to others who they imagine themselves to be, why they say the things they say and act the things they act, can certainly bring home to its followers a clearer vision of why in a group dynamics session they carry on as they do, it is quite fanciful to imagine that this new understanding also equips them to master the imperious demands of external and objective responsibility.

Task-oriented accountability penetrates the human secrets more deeply than wiping off the grease paint of higher education. Although it would be uncharitable to insist that this, too, might lack all virtues. But Action Learning is more than detergent; it insists upon keeping to a sequenced timetable, observing the iron disciplines of an industrial or commercial setting, with penalties for not achieving such-and-such by times agreed beforehand.

Such exercises as sensitivity training, non-directive counselling and other excursions into group psychotherapy are but rarely anchored to the here-and-now demands of business. This, of course, is not to say that they are inferior to the re-interpretations of past experience and of present qualities – or even of future hopes – necessarily urged upon the subject by Action Learning. It may well be that, in preparation for responsibility involving the external world as well as committing oneself, one ought to begin by trying to identify the misunderstandings generated by the self and only later take on the ambiguities of that same external world. My own opinion is that the two sources of error are far from separable; I should hesitate to join any discussion that tried to mark where my world left off and I began.

Insofar as all of this is to be secured without serious responsibility for improving, on a basis laid down by others, some external and independent reality, it cannot be assimilated to Action Learning. Nevertheless, in following some of these movements the participants may become so much more aware of the effects they are having upon other persons, that they ask themselves how they might also have more influence upon the objective world in which they and those others need to exist. If this were so, then the movements referred to will serve as overtures to Action Learning.

CONSULTANCY AND OTHER EXPERT MISSIONS

It is frequently said by top managers that, were they ever inclined to ask themselves if there might be problems or opportunities deserving their attention other than those continuously arising from the daily round, they would at once send for some reputable firm of business consultants – company doctors, management professors, experts from Boston, confidential advisers, and so forth.

The idea that what might be lacking is something personal to the top managers themselves, something, moreover, that they alone might one day be able to put right, would strike them as very strange. It would be even stranger to them to suggest that, not only were they themselves alone in being able to put things right, but that only they, too, could discover the avenues to successful amendment.

But since there can be no learning without action and no action without learning (if change is to be brought about by the purchased services of outsiders, independently of any involvement at a personal level of the top managers who commission those outsiders) then there can be no learning – that is, no preparation among those at present in charge to meet the recurrent challenges of the future.

The enterprise will therefore become dependent upon its external advisers until it can no longer afford to meet their fees and expenses – a condition now frequently encountered. Nor is this all. The external consultant generally claims expertise in such-and-such a field, and, on this account, will diagnose the affliction (or interpret the hope) of their client management in terms of it. For a month or more everything will go as predicted, the pattern uncovered will fit the forecast already made, and the plan of action will build upon the personal enthusiasms of members of the host management. The outside consultants who have prepared the plan – not seldom by piecing together fragments of their past prescriptions to other clients – will gradually "phase themselves out", leaving those on the spot to implement what still needs to be done.

With their wide connections across a fast professional culture, the itinerant experts are able quickly to find the super-specialist needed (it might seem) to advise upon some highly technical obstruction to success. The very speed and certainty with which these talents are specified, recruited and deployed will ensure that no single member of the host management will learn much from their involvement.

The assignment of a visiting participant from another enterprise also anxious to do something about its more obstinate and ill-structured embarrassments has little in common with the engagement of professional experts. Were the participants of the Belgian inter-university programme to carry visiting cards to widen their possibilities of future employment, they would endorse them in red capitals: "Our strength, just like your own, lies in our ignorance of your troubles."

For, while the expert may pretend that her first desire is to see the problem as it is seen by the management that needs to do something about it, she is in this particular business for a quite different reason. The visiting participant, on the other hand, is clearly another manager in fact, anxious to interpret the trouble as a manager among managers, and to learn from their hosts as much as they are to learn from him. They do not seek to prolong their engagement with their hosts, or to withhold unpleasant advice that may prejudice the willingness of his clients to meet their financial obligations – since there are none. They are not hoping, as are many consultants, that they may be offered an appointment in the firm they are setting out to help, so that their advice will not be coloured by quite adventitious possibilities having nothing to do at all with the original reasons for their being in the Action Learning programme.

Faced with a temporary check, the visiting participant has no headquarters office they may ring for instant support from another itinerant expert. Instead they will need to open up some fresh line of questioning with their hosts. Unlike the professional consultant, they will not be spending a lot of their time trying to find out what the most powerful person in the receiving organization believes the problem to be in order to present to them a solution based upon that interpretation. The visiting participant will, laboriously and with little thanks, be trying to reconcile the myriad views and experiences of large numbers of their new colleagues in such a manner that these now start to suggest what might be going on and how it may be improved upon.

While in practice the expert consultant is desperately striving to use every interview they conduct as a means of assembling every shred of an idea from others into what they will claim as their own solution, they must be very cautious about creating the impression that they are circulating as the thirstiest of learners. Their official status is a teller of others, an instructor of babes, a guide to the foolish, an enlightener dispelling the darkness, a leader of the blind, and so forth. They must be extremely cautious about giving an impression that there is anything they have to learn.

The visiting participant, on the other hand, gets the authority to help their new colleagues from their own eagerness to learn by recording the explanations of what these colleagues themselves imagine to be wrong. As the supreme non-expert, they are, at least at the outset, in no position to question what others say, nor to stem their desire to say it – and hence to learn from what others are trying to tell them about that which, they feel, seems to pass their own understanding.

As St Paul reminded us all: "Let no man deceive himself. If any man among you seemeth to be wise in this world, let him become a fool that he may be wise." (1 *Corinthians* ch.3 v.18) It is one of the texts upon which Action Learning is founded, but rarely seen on the Christmas cards from experts.

OPERATIONAL RESEARCH, INDUSTRIAL ENGINEERING, WORK STUDY AND RELATED SUBJECTS

Action Learning will make extensive use of all or any of the technical methods that have been so ingeniously developed by these subjects over the past forty years. And as time goes on, and they absorb the study of subjective judgment, so the approaches taken by the true thinkers in these fields will become closer to those of Action Learning.

It must always be a question as to how far the exploration of the purely random, that is now the epistemological core of Action Learning (how best to explore one's residual ignorance in the light of what others may have to suggest), will be admitted as a legitimate annexe to the supposedly exact sciences, and their associated technologies.

All seems to turn upon one's starting point; the manager, tormented by the need to get something done, is just as likely to admit inspired guesswork to their counsels as they are all manner of quantitative analysis, since the second may be useless without the first – like throwing a life belt on the strongest of nylon lines one hundred feet long to the drowning man one hundred and five feet away. The professional analyst, on the other hand, may feel that the exploration by subjective means – trial and error, conjecture and refutation, Action Learning – is unscientific, so that all seaside resorts should make their lifelines at least one hundred and five feet long. It remains to be seen.

Many years ago, the physicists accepted uncertainty as a fact of existence, and Werner Heisenberg is seen as one of the greatest among their number. Action Learning is still largely ignored by the operational research workers and their associates, probably in the belief that, as the computer becomes ever faster and more capacious, it will absorb the margins of managerial uncertainties within its spreading range.

There is little point in arguing the matter, but I am sure they will one day need to follow the example of the physicists – if for very different reasons. The Book of Proverbs told us all 2,500 years ago that the future is uncertain: "Boast not thyself of tomorrow; for thou knowest not what a day may bring forth." (*Proverbs* ch.27 v.1) Although Action Learning cannot pretend to foresee the future, it may, by helping anybody likely to encounter it understand more clearly who they think they are, also enable them more realistically to cope with it when it arrives.

Simple common sense

One is frequently told that Action Learning is no more –

and cannot possibly be any more – than the simplest common sense.

When the innocent non-expert sees that the questions of the traditionalist obscure from her the simplest of truths, and when, after she has been able to overcome their objections to some fresh approach, she succeeds, against all their professional ridicule and sophisticated detraction in achieving the goal they are able conclusively to prove impossible, she must then face her second trial: of being told that all she did was simple common sense.

It is enough to use popular illustrations; first, in the story of David and Goliath; second, in the chronicles of Christopher Columbus. As to the first: the Israelites are trapped against the rock by the Philistines and are in danger, after forty days, of dying from thirst; they are pinned there by the armoured giant, their expertise. No bigger Israelite, with thicker armour and heavier spear, exists, and so there is no other way out for the experts. But David, who has never worn armour and never fought in a battle, sees that the problem is to ask a different question. It is no longer: "Where do we find a bigger man to conquer Goliath?", but: "Granted that there is and can be no bigger man, how otherwise do we get rid of Goliath?"

Even after he had seen this to be the proper question, David had to reject the smallest suit of armour in the camp, ordered by King Saul to be put upon him. And then, when Goliath lay dead, there must have been those Israelites who remarked: "Well, what's all the fuss about? Simply because this boy gets a pebble from the brook and hits Goliath between the eyes… Why, any fool can think of things like that! What is it, after all, but simple common sense."

And as to the second; Columbus hears the courtiers on about where he had got to. "All he had to do was get in a boat – not even his own, mark you! Then he hoists the sail and waits to see what happens. He finds land – so he says – rests for a few days and then comes back. Why, any fool can do that! What on earth's all the fuss about?"

So Columbus suggests they should attempt to stand an egg on end; then try all evening but none succeeds, even although Columbus assures them it is possible. After most have admitted they cannot do what he says he knows how to, they demand that he demonstrates his elusive skill. He gives the egg a sharp tap, lightly crushing the end and it remains erect. There is a howl of execration, such as only experts are capable of howling – although not necessarily under provocation. "Well, of course, if you do it like that! It stands to reason. What's all the fuss? Any fool can think of that! Why, its only common sense, after all!" And so on and so forth, without limit. We're all experts.

True common sense, also known as wisdom, is rarely displayed by experts of any kind, particularly when explaining why their expertise prevents them from seeing the simplest of truths. If by "common sense" wisdom is implied, and Action Learning dismissed as mere common sense, then we have reason to feel flattered, for this is as Action Learning should be seen. It sets out to explore what one does not know, and why one does not know it, for the wise person is more interested in what they cannot see of their troubles than in what they can.

There may be a lot more in Action Learning than can be dismissed as mere common sense. On the other hand, both may be no more than the ability to ask unusual questions.

WHY ACTION LEARNING DIFFERS

We conclude this Chapter with the remark that Action Learning is less structured than these other approaches, which have long been associated with particular schools and identifiable philosophers.

Since it is less structured, like space and time themselves, it is available to all persons and may be all things to all people. Since it must follow the very wide variety of managerial practice that it is intended to improve, and since it has no syllabus of its own, there is little wonder that everybody who does not understand it must at once assert that they have been doing it for donkey's years.

It makes little use of teachers, specialist and other professional sclerotics, and tries to encourage the managers themselves, those who have to take the decisions about their own tasks, to discover who best to help each other.

Whereas we may liken the traditional management schools, and the great supermarket of academic packages they have on offer, to a coterie of fashionable clubs served by world-renowned bartenders, each secretly dispensing their scholarly ambrosias, we can liken Action Learning to no more than the managers gallantly drinking each others health in cold water at the factory tap. At least, they are not paying through the nose for a regime of self-deception.

7. Experiences of Launching Action Learning

IN THIS CHAPTER: An abstract of initiations world-wide.

Contents

* NOTE: It is now many years since the first printed report recommended
Action Learning – one to The Mining Association of Great Britain, the pre-
War owners of the coal industry, in October 1945, suggesting a staff college
for those with problems to come together and learn with and from each
other, a venture that did not envisage the permanent employment of a highly
qualified staff of specialist tutors to deliver the lectures or conduct the
seminars. The staff college would bring together groups of persons interested
in common problems, who, under a leader taken from within the industry
and previously invited to introduce a subject, or under a succession of such
leaders, would be prepared to spend a weekend, a week, or a fortnight, or
even in special cases perhaps longer, on the fullest interchange of their ideas
and experiences of those problems. See also Bibliography below.

7 Experiences of Launching Action Learning

It is probably because the earliest statement of the nature of Action Learning* - from the diagnosis and treatment of real problems in the company of comrades in adversity rather than from the reminiscences of no-longer-involved experts - was seen from the outset as uncompromisingly opposed to the interests of academics that it has taken so long for the idea to catch on. The extent and nature of this catching-on, what is more, are by no means so clear as the recommendations made first in 1945 were intended to imply. Much now on the market as Action Learning would not be easy to identify as such by those who have spent the time since then in following its fight for recognition.

For this reason it may be helpful to describe the steps by which some of the pioneers have managed to get programmes established so far - never forgetting that, "The race is not to the swift, nor the battle to the strong, neither yet bread to the wise, nor yet riches to men of understanding, nor yet favour to men of skill; but time and chance happeneth to them all." (*Ecclesiastes* ch.9 v.11) Little can be guaranteed by following the advice of others, set out on the distant pages of a book. Nevertheless, the identifiable stages seem to be these:

EARLY RUMOURS

One may come across some public reference to Action Learning, probably by some other name, such as management action, experiential development, group activity training and over fifty others. All depend upon the simple idea of some real and assigned task as the syllabus, and the regular confrontation with a few equals as the medium; even if it is partly concealed between the constant supervision of some facilitator who attends the confrontations, and the packaged course of lectures given by experts, without particular relevance to the varied assignments that are the foundation of the programme.

Whatever the reference, something attracts the attention of a manager who may seek further information from a local management school or institute of management. In GEC the first contact was from the managing director (then Sir Arnold Weinstock) who saw the writer on a television programme, and made touch through the BBC. Since the educational press has given little attention to the subject - and pursues an expert policy of not reviewing the writer's own books - it is rare for first contacts to come from the established literature.

INFORMED ACQUAINTANCE

It is generally essential to follow up the early rumours, and the first contacts to which they may be expected to lead. It is very easy for those who seek a new light to be led firmly towards the old, and they will be well advised to ask pretty quickly those offering to sell them Action Learning a few simple questions.

The first of these should discover how the salesman

earned a living yesterday, and whether they have made any contribution to the development of Action Learning, corroborated, if possible, by the managers in the real world identified as having gained from these earlier exercises. There are now several channels through which potential participants can secure reliable endorsements of any agencies offering to run Action Learning programmes for them, including many of those currently referred to in the Bibliography. It is, unfortunately, necessary to make these uncharitable comments about the transition from early rumours to informed acquaintance, since Action Learning could scarcely have taken more than a generation to become established in the country of its origin had not it been seen as a threat to those doing well out of established courses.

The danger is now different; an early interest in Action Learning, instead of being suppressed by the opinions of experts as being "unscientific", will now be welcomed - to be deflected into something claimed by other experts to be more up-to-date and "more fully staffed".

ACTIVE MOTIVATION

No organization is likely to embrace Action Learning unless there is some person within it ready to fight on it behalf.

Careful observation suggests that it is rarely a conviction about the merits of Action Learning as such that first inclines people to take it up. Only when they become convinced that their existing approaches to managerial and supervisory training are not likely to get anywhere will they turn to the untried and the challenging. Since the last persons to admit that existing development schemes fall below desirable standards are those who run them, it is rare for the active motivation to start with the personnel department, or with the chief training officer, who probably owe their present seniority to having built up a system now under attack. Their instincts are to jump to its defence - one way to protect their established edifice is to disparage whatever may challenge it, and, when Action Learning is imperfectly understood, it can very quickly be disparaged.

Inspiring and motivating can thus be a tricky business. The key seems to be in making an ally of some powerful member of the coalition of power responsible for the organization and, from the earliest possible moment, contriving that this person and the head of training work closely together. This dialogue is sometimes started directly by the training staff, after it has become known to them that the coalition of power is beginning to have reservations about training budgets and the like. It is sometimes started by a managing director, or senior engineer, or even an industrial relations officer, who has learned from a professional colleague in another enterprise that Action Learning may have something going for it.

This useful intermediary we may call the *accoucheur* - the managerial midwife who sees that their organization gives birth to a new idea, without themselves needing to attest either its past origins or its future nourishment in any professional sense. It would be instructive to make a content analysis of the missions of the last hundred *accoucheurs*, to discover how they first got worked up, what they said to the training staff, how they put the idea to colleagues on the board - or elsewhere at the top - and how their own views of what they were up to changed as they advanced.

One managing director, forced to concentrate on Action Learning as the last hope for saving his twelve hundred strong business, has not only recorded how he did this, but has set up an Action Learning centre on his retirement. If he, personally, is not able to convince a few other line or operational managers in other enterprises that they might join their training managers as the factory or enterprise *accoucheurs*, so as to concentrate a few top level minds on making a fresh start on their chronic troubles, we shall need to abandon hope altogether and to write off whatsoever is left.

CONSTRUCTIVE LOBBYING

Experience suggests that many months may elapse between recruiting the *accoucheur* to team up with the personnel and training staff, and securing a final decision from the coalition of power to start any programme of substance. The *accoucheur* must, of course, be a politically mature person, well able to pilot any ideas they believe in through the troubled waters that surge around the board room and other refuges.

It will be long before those now trying to promote Action Learning will be able specifically to develop these key supporters. In due course, no doubt, as those now participating in Action Learning programmes secure the promotions they deserve, they will carry to the higher levels of their employment the beliefs they are now acquiring - especially if, as in other countries, the quality of the Action Learning projects reach such standards that their analysis and documentation may well form the dissertations for higher degrees. But, for the present, such preparatory overtures are unknown in Britain. [This is now no longer the case. The Revans Centre for Action Learning and Research at Salford University offers postgraduate degree and diploma programmes to those engaged in Action Learning, as do some other higher education institutions in the UK and elsewhere. (MJP)]

Either the enterprise has one or two potential *accoucheurs* among its top people or it has not, and, if they are lacking, it seems that the only means of inspiring others to assume the role is through the professional institutions, by addressing their conferences in the hope that some line manager will ask a few questions and find him- or herself referred to a colleague in another enterprise known to be convinced that action learning has helped in some other context.

It is certainly through some operational need, felt and identified (if not accurately diagnosed) by some line department, that the *accoucheur* will most effectively diffuse their new enthusiasm among the small band of allies always needed to start anything afresh. It should be the professional responsibility of the training staff to see that they are properly supplied with all they need to interest their other colleagues, including introductions to those from other enterprises - or even local authorities and public corporations - who can describe convincingly what Action Learning has done to help them with their own practical problems elsewhere.

How this game of micro-politics is played is, of course, up to the *accoucheur,* who will be wise to listen carefully to such outsiders. Above all, the opportunity for them to interest the coalition of power in actually getting a programme started with the maximum of support must be left to their political judgment.   Such an occasion might have nothing whatsoever to do with discussions about training policy or development budgets. It is most likely to arise during the discussion of some obstinate affliction, when the coalition is as aware as it possibly can be of the seriousness of the trouble and of the inadequacy of their attacks upon it.

The occasion can always be taken for the board to invite, through the *accoucheur*, the member or members (potential clients) most tormented by the problem to talk it over with the counterpart from the other firm known to the *accoucheur* to have met with success - or with such as the former managing director who actually saved his enterprise from closure. But, as in all Action Learning, our problem is not only to find *accoucheurs*: it is to keep them in touch with those genuinely able to help them from personal conviction and successful experience.

TOP MANAGEMENT DECISION

The intrigues of the *accoucheur* and their professional accomplice from the training staff must be looked upon as merely a cultural preparation: they will not, of themselves, ensure that the coalition of power will actually decide to do anything. The notion that something new and different needs to be done is no easy one to implant where it needs to be implanted, at the very top of the organization.

Early experience, among the colliery managers and the hospital administrations where the first consortia were set up so long ago, suggested that those in charge of a unit are much more likely to face the risks of innovation if several of them can be got together to stimulate each other to think afresh. Just as the Action Learning set of five or so participants striving to make sense each of their own projects endow one another with unsuspected skill and courage, so the representatives of different top managements coming together at the invitation of one of them are much more likely to play the dare-devil than if they are, in some fashion, enticed singly into the minefields of discovery.

If all of those who turn up are thoroughly aware that their organizations can no longer vacillate but must do something quite novel, each will understand enough of the conundrums faced by the others to contribute to the total discussion the encouragement to take studied risks, even sufficient to tip the scales held teetering by one party present. What is, in fact, happening at such a confabulation - for the risks known to be involved soon give the exchanges a most personal and even single-minded quality - is that, exactly as in the formal set discussion, all are helping the others to perceive their necessities afresh.

A much wider range of lived experience is being invoked, simply because it is there to be invoked, and it happens to be the very kind of lived experience so badly needed: that of other real top managers accumulated from their past attempts to do something about other troubles, some of which may have presented elements like those now tormenting others around the table. However this may be, it was the constant discussion about their real troubles among the presidents of the large Belgian enterprises, more than any intellectual explanation from the academics and training experts, that led to most final decisions to go ahead. There is similar evidence (in 1982 and later) that such mutual support in risk-taking will also help British industry and commerce to make a long-delayed beginning.

What will probably be decisive in the long run is the extent to which top managements themselves will take these launching initiatives. Unless the appeal for support comes from some other coalition of power as a personal touch, it is unlikely to get very far. We are deceiving ourselves if we imagine that the most precious asset top management commands - its lived experience, deep and often hard to discover - is going to become available for wider use unless that top management is itself to become personally involved in offering it to others.

Thus it is that those anxious to persuade coalitions of power to tackle their troubles by Action Learning should recognise the need first to get the coalitions of power exchanging confidences among themselves.

OPERATIONAL DESIGN

The top management, once it has chosen from a list of three or four vexatious troubles that on which it is ready to make a start, must decide in what way it can make known throughout its dominions that it is seriously committed to the new approach.

The move to develop a spirit of question-posing in a hierarchical system traditionally run by experts is sometimes met with alarm by its middle managers, since, if they are allowed to ask questions of their superiors, there will be a danger of foremen and supervisors being permitted to ask questions of their own departmental heads.

The most simple and effective way to prepare the operational managers is to meet them altogether, or, where the institution works around the clock, like a hospital or colliery, in large numbers shift by shift. It is important that all subordinate managers should be able to hear the kinds of responses made by their colleagues to the suggestion that all in the hierarchy are being invited to work together on whatsoever problems are thrown up. Unless the majority of the staff are convinced that their coalition of power is in real earnest, the co-operation given to the Action Learning participants will be less than may be necessary.

Nor is this all. The finest way to get the circulation going among the middle management is for them to be convinced that those at the top, too, are trying to make better use of the resources available to them. Precisely what manner of departmental meetings, too, may be called for to ensure more open exchanges between those likely to become involved in the diagnosis and therapy will need to be worked out as the client and the helpers get started. The important need is to ensure, by public presentation, that the top wants something done and is ready to play a new part in helping to do it.

Those at the higher levels may sometimes be surprised by the responses they get: foremen and middle managers willing to work long hours in their own time without payment; offers to run a newsletter keeping everybody in the picture; suggestions about local projects, designed to add detail to the wider investigations inspired from above; and requests for further general meetings after some of the middle managers have got together to work out a timetable for their own supplementary service groups.

PREPARATORY WORKSHOPS

Once all the above steps have been taken, perhaps with the help of some local or regional management centre, the staff of some already experienced firm or internationally recognised authority, it will be time to run some kind of introductory seminar or workshop for those within the organization likely to become engaged.

As far as possible, the ideas of this book should be available to the key persons among these, since there is no harm in the fundamental nature of Action Learning becoming a topic of discussion in the light of what the organization is trying to do. And, moreover, the specific roles that need to be filled, client and client group, sponsor, participant and, where one is needed, set launcher or set adviser, should be described by a real manager who has actually gone through the real and responsible experience of tackling urgent and threatening problems.

The ready mark that they have done so is their ability to take the obscure and ill-framed questions of those about to tackle Action Learning for the first time, and to distil from them at least half-a-dozen major issues, all dimly forming in the mind of the questioners. But, although all may be managers of the same rank and professional qualification, the one will have spent several months in the company of three or four others learning how to explore his or her own ignorance through the enlightenment of needing to do something about it, and in such a way as to avoid deceiving themselves about the consequences.

Moreover, the real manager who has actually been through such a programme will, not unlike a Catherine Wheel, throw off all manner of comment about their own adventures, and return to their inquisitors all levels of questions - some extremely personal - so that his or her own delight in the exchanges is more than apparent. It becomes, in practice, a learning experience for the older hand; they are, to some extent, reliving what they have been through, and all the better for it.

These preparatory workshops should, as far as possible, involve the future participants from more than one enterprise, even although this may be a very large one, with problems enough to run self-contained Action Learning programmes on its own. Those who attend it should be expected to have read the first two sections of this booklet, or to have acquainted themselves with the aims and the methods of Action Learning from other sources. It is important that this should be required of the participants, in order that time is not wasted over the need to convince them - as all on first hearing need to be convinced - that Action Learning is fundamentally different from most other educational experience.

Grown men and women usually encounter with utter incredulity the suggestion, first put to them, that it is from their own experience of the past and their own uncertainties about the future they are now to learn. They cannot believe that they are not to copy down in their best handwriting what some professor is throwing from an overhead projector upon the classroom wall in front of them, nor to act through some charade with all taking parts as managers, shop-stewards, foremen welders and so forth, in order to put across the principles of cognitive dissonance or sapiential authority. The notion that constructive activity will be expected from those on the floor of the workshop can be highly disturbing, not only to the teaching profession but also to the participants. They should be prepared before they come to meet each other for the first time. . . . Years of educational inertia are looking down on us.

The workshop should last at least a couple of days, so that the participants can sleep on the ideas first put to them, and thereby become initiated into the habit of posing questions they have had the chance to think out for themselves. Its agenda need not be rigidly framed in advance, since the participants - should things go properly - will have all kinds of suggestions to make about diagnosing and treating the troubles billed to be attacked.

Perhaps the most difficult idea to get across at this first gathering is the dependence of the whole project for its success upon all trying to discover what needs to be done - including how most effectively to use the time of the workshop to decide the future course of action. It is most faithfully to engender this critically positive approach that the presence of real managers from elsewhere who have themselves gone through their own Action Learning experiences can be so stimulating. A second get-together should be suggested, to be staged for a half-day six weeks later, in order that all may be able to report back how they are getting on and what else might need to be done to make sure that all the key participants fully understand what is to be expected of them.

EXCHANGING EXPERIENCES OF LAUNCHING ACTION LEARNING

For the next few years, while Action Learning is still emerging from the authoritarianism of traditional education - being told by experts how to become proficient in yesterday's receding pastimes - it will help the whole movement if fairly accurate records are made of what goes on at these preparatory workshops.

We know much less than we think we do about how to stimulate responsible people to put their energies into making a better job of what they are supposed to be doing, and there is nothing like encouraging them to find out for themselves how a better job might be done. We could all get quite a lot out of exchanging among ourselves the impressions we have of how things are successfully (or unsuccessfully) launched, and there is an important task to be tackled here by the training staffs of the organizations that try launching them.

The political acuity of the *accoucheur* will be sufficient to make them realise at a fairly early stage their own need for information and advice as to what Action Learning may be, at a level more profound than can ever be expressed in the literature, or even in conversation with a former participant. For this reason - and because, in accordance with the tenets of Action Learning, *accoucheurs* are likely to learn anything worth knowing only from other *accoucheurs* - workshops can be held at which the tasks of the *accoucheurs* can be offered for analysis and development by the *accoucheurs* themselves. At such convocations the following matters would all find a place on the agenda:

- choice of problems around which to form projects
- roles and responsibilities of clients
- qualities and selection of participants
- representation of the organization in any consortium
- monitoring of projects
- development of set advisers
- role of training staffs
- induction of participants into their projects
- continued support of participants
- continuing role of line management in the projects
- supply of appropriate technical knowledge
- autonomous extension of projects into other projects

- issues of cost and benefit
- concept of the whole organization as a learning system.

8. The Enterprise as a Learning System

IN THIS CHAPTER: The conditions for bringing about learning in the organization as a whole system.

Contents

*NOTE: This chapter, which has not been part of the *ABC of Action Learning* before, has been selected and added by the General Editor. Written in 1969 whilst Revans was working in Brussels it was first published as "The Enterprise as a Learning System" in Revans R W (1982) *The Origins and Growth of Action Learning* (MJP) (see Bibliography)

8 The Enterprise as a Learning System[*]

It had been discovered that the presence of a visiting manager within an enterprise whose management had become convinced of the need for a lot of those employed there to learn, particularly when supported by a band of allies, could in fact engender an enlightenment previously unsuspected.

Our key assumption was that the presence within each enterprise of an outsider undisguised, simply behaving as the intelligent learner about some problem he or she had never before encountered, soon set off a secondary, but nevertheless powerful, campaign of learning among the staff on the spot and with whom they regularly discussed their lines of enquiry.

Since the visitor was not only trying to understand their own approach to conditions of ignorance, risk and confusion, but was also the agent of the home management equally concerned to make sense of what appeared to them an intractable difficulty, a very simple question arose: Was the secondary (autonomous) learning process engendered merely because the majority of subordinates had become aware that the problem existed, and that it was seen by their top management to be serious? Or, was the visitor more than an agent, in the sense that without them there could not possibly have started any autonomous curiosity among the home staff at all?

If there is, in most organizations staffed with normally

intelligent persons, a latent desire to behave sensibly in front of colleagues (as the visiting participants of the programme seemed to have discovered) could this desire not be identified and turned to constructive use without needing to go through the elaborate ceremonies of exchanging senior managers?

If the enterprise was, in fact, already a potential learning system, could its capacity for self-development be exploited autonomously by the top management taking the lead? Why, except when the learning of the senior managers was the cardinal objective, do more than get the local staffs and their existing people running their own enquiries?

Alas, the suggestion was grossly premature. It was rejected even by those who had had the courage to open their secrets to the exchanges of the Belgian inter-university programme. Not until the Japanese menace of the late 1970s introduced the Q-circle to Europe, could the issue once more be raised.

THE ENTERPRISE AS A SYSTEM OF SYSTEMS

Many persons concerned with the business enterprise, whether as a director, employee or adviser, will have their own professional reasons for perceiving it as some manner of system.

For example, the controller, who needs to ensure that its total revenue exceeds, one year with another, its total expenditure, without the specific costs of such-and-such a department necessarily being met by its own specific income; the manufacturing superintendent, who will expect some overall balance between its flow of goods and materials, not being embarrassed at one moment by a chronic shortage of stock to meet the orders, nor at another by a sharp reminder that too much capital is tied up in a superabundance of raw materials; the personnel director, who hopes that, five years hence, the enterprise will still be able to rely upon 80 per cent of the staff now serving it, each and every one richer by five intervening years of precious experience .

All these senior people, to ensure continuity and balanced effectiveness, need to think in terms of inputs, flows and outputs. None must envisage the enterprise as a series of isolated and independent jerks of activity, springing at random into local effect and unrelated to any larger and continuous totality.

Such systemic approaches would be readily claimed by most departmental heads. To ensure such organic thinking, there exists a vast range of professional teaching and qualification, embracing such arts as budgetary control and standard costing, production scheduling and inventory control, manpower planning and staff development, and an inexhaustible army of managerial techniques marching in acronymic procession across the prospectuses of business schools - PERT, CPA, DCF, TWI, MBO, OD, OR, X or Y, and a score of others.

THE INDIVIDUAL AND THE TASK

Such unifying ideas arouse little contention. They have indeed entered deeply into the planning both of the working organizations themselves and the many educational programmes enticing managers to think of their firms or departments as "systems" with many interacting parts. It would hardly be rash to suggest that one third of all published management literature is concerned with such issues of functional organization, nor that an even larger proportion of time is devoted to them on management courses.

But there is now evidence that, however useful, however valid, may be this functional approach, the concept of the enterprise as a system has quite other but no less significant interpretations. The tasks that every person carries out in the course of their daily employment, whether at first sight concerned with purchasing, design, manufacture, marketing, transport, accountancy, personnel development or wages payment, contain another systemic element, the potential power of which is only of late becoming recognised. As the chief executive of one of Britain's largest firms remarked:

"Our main concern is no longer to ensure that we find, train and keep the biggest share of Britain's leading chemists, nor is it solely to concentrate on the maximum return on our investment. These are necessary ends, but of themselves are insufficient. Our need in the 1970s is to see ourselves as a developing system of two hundred thousand individuals."

A DIGRESSION ON MANAGEMENT TECHNIQUES

We see there is little new in this expression of need. Almost the same sentiment was declared by Robert Owen a century and a half ago. Similar things are said in Europe and by Chairman Mao. But we do not here interpret the enterprise as a human system in the light of this nor that political doctrine.

Not are we suggesting the need for some super-system, stored in a giant computer, to which the controls of orders, purchases, production, quality, cost and so forth, alike report. For in whatever political system, whether in the countries of the OECD, in Eastern Europe or in the Third World, we now observe some impatience with - indeed a revolt against - the systematising experts who, during the past century, have over-regulated the tasks of people at all levels.

Industrial engineering, work study, incentive payment schemes, task specialisation, time tabling and scheduling and, above all, the machine pacing of human work, are now held up as a caricature of Charlie Chaplin's *Modern Times*, and all carry within them the seeds of their own destruction in proportion to the authority of the experts who exploit them. The latest casualty amongst these managerial bailiffs is, it seems, productivity bargaining. This rigmarole of wage assessment, exalted some years ago into the very diadem of behavioural science, was subsequently appraised by some jaundiced personnel expert as a dead duck.

THE ENTERPRISE AS A LEARNING SYSTEM

We observe that all expert systems here referred to must now be imposed upon the enterprise from above or from outside. But Action Learning must seek the means of improvement from within, indeed from the common task.

An essential quality of human behaviour is that, although in some degree innate or inherited, it is in great part learned. Present conduct is largely our visible response to past experience newly interpreted. It follows first, that the daily round offers constant learning opportunities and, second, that these opportunities should be of great interest to managers. When moreover, we discover that the quality of such learning is largely determined by the morale of the organization that offers it, the interest becomes profound.

Indeed we may now assert that the observable differences between organizations otherwise comparable in technical, financial or environmental character, are determined by whether or not their members are likely to develop in and from the course of their daily employment.

One enterprise can, in short, behave as a learning system, constantly and fruitfully working out autonomous solutions to its own problems. Its neighbour, built to the same technical specifications, engaged in the same tasks and reporting to the same higher authority, may be an organizational sore, running with irresolvable conflict and unendurable frustration. [See further, *The Origins and Growth of Action Learning* noted in the Bibliography below].

It is thus to the enterprise as a learning system that we need to attend. We must understand how it is that one management can continuously act to encourage such an elevation of the spirit, while their colleagues across the way live under constant threat from their own subordinates.

THE QUALITIES OF AUTONOMOUS LEARNING SYSTEMS

Our research evidence to suggest whether or not its management policies are likely to develop an enterprise as an autonomous learning system may still be incomplete. But the conditions for success seem to include the following.

> 1 Chief executives place high among their own responsibilities that of developing the enterprise as a learning system.

This he or she will achieve through their personal relations with their immediate staff, since the conduct of one level of a system towards any level below it is powerfully influenced by the perception that the higher level has of its treatment from above.

In one consortium of hospitals the correlation between systematic development (attitudinal change, learning) and interest of top management was +0.91. In the secondary modern schools of Lancashire the correlation between the estimates made by the children of their teachers' skills, on the one hand, and their assessment of them as approachable human beings, on the other, was +0.87. [See further, *The Origins and Growth of Action Learning,* noted in the Bibliography below].

Both of these add a veneer of quantitative cunning to the immemorial verse: "As the judge of the people is, so are his officers; and what manner of man the ruler of a city is himself, so are all they that inhabit therein." (*Ecclesiasticus* ch.10 v. 2)

2 The coalition of power that runs the enterprise has clear ideas about delegation, with the maximum authority for staff to act within the field of its own known policies that become known by interrogation from below.

Systems of delegation, in other words, are constantly worked out as part of the contract between the person, the task and their superior. The success of delegation depends significantly upon the quality of data/information made available. In one experimental enterprise the correlation among fifty graduate senior managers between the perceived quality of their information system, on the one hand, and their own personal satisfactions as departmental managers, on the other, was $+0.78$.

3 Codes of practice, standard rules and procedures, works orders and other such regulations, in consequence, are to be seen as norms around which variations are deliberately encouraged as learning opportunities.

These will therefore contribute to the improvement of the data/information flow and may even bring into a common learning experience different members of an organization who, under codes rigorously observed, might rarely, if ever, meet.

4 Any reference of what appears an intractable problem to a superior level should be accompanied both by an explanation of why it cannot be treated where it seems to have arisen and a proposal to change the system so that similar problems arising in future could be suitably contained and treated.

5 Persons at all levels should be encouraged, with their immediate colleagues to make regular proposals for the study and re-organization of their own systems of work.

Such proposals should generate discussion between vertical levels and horizontal departments of how the work is currently managed, and of how its outcome is determined, such as the content, order and distribution of individual tasks, the use and maintenance of equipment and supplies, and the flow of information essential to performing the tasks. Above all, in any suggestions about the reorganization of the work, first attention should be given to its group or autonomous aspects. [See further, *The Origins and Growth of Action Learning* noted in the Bibliography below].

AUTONOMOUS LEARNING NOT MANAGERIAL ABDICATION

A management that interprets the employment of its staff as a continuous opportunity for their self-development, does not, by setting aside the mythologies of "scientific management" about commanding, co-ordinating and controlling, thereby resign to the under-strappers all responsibility for running the enterprise. It merely acknowledges that the enterprise is the setting in which the staff spend most of their active lives, and that the total contract between it and its employees is wider than an agreement about who is to be paid for doing what.

The wider bargain, even if not explicit, has deep implications for personal development and personal autonomy. Outstanding persons should be encouraged to develop themselves to the limits of their capacities and ought not to be restricted entirely by ingenious mechanistic programmes devised by quick-witted experts trained not to ask questions outside their own fields.

Indeed, the present relation between those who perform and those who plan calls often to be stood upon its head - it is for the individual worker, as a member of a wealth creating group, to suggest their optimum conditions of work and to set their personal standards of achievement; and for the expert to solve (with the help of the group) whatever problems the worker may introduce.

Such new approaches to work organization will offer management their own opportunities to learn; they are certainly no invitation to staff to take over and run the whole show. Some senior managers may, of course, offer to take over, or even to buy out from the main shareholders, their section of the total enterprise; this will be a measure of the present need of the enterprise to learn.

The most precious asset of any organization is the one most readily overlooked: its capacity to build upon its lived experience, to learn from its challenges and to turn in a better performance by inviting all and sundry to work out for themselves what that performance ought to be.

Bibliography

FOUR KEY WORKS

Reg Revans has written eloquently over many years about Action Learning. His books repay repeated study. Unfortunately most of these are now out of print and must be had from libraries, especially those at the Revans Centre for Action Learning & Research and IFAL (See below for details). Four books by Revans in particular chart the development of the Action Learning idea:

Developing Effective Managers (1971) Praeger, New York

> Based on the Belgian exchange programme which had such an enduring impact on his thinking, this book stands as the most formal attempt to develop a theory of action learning via the detailed exposition of three interacting systems:

> Alpha - *the decision or strategy system* which rests on the managers' values, the external environment and the available internal resources;

> Beta - *the influencing or negotiation* cycle required to implement the decision or strategy - of survey, trial, action, audit and consolidation; and

Gamma - *the learning process* as experienced uniquely by each action learner, involving self-questioning and awareness of self and others.

Revans' summary view is that "System gamma was the essence, .. (it) .. represents in its own way the structure of all intelligent behaviour, and offers in conjunction with systems alpha and beta, one starting point for a general theory of human action, for a science of praxeology." (p58)

Action Learning: New Techniques for Managers (1980) Blond and Briggs, London

A four part odyssey which demonstrates the width and depth of Revans' thinking. Part 1 consists of nine Action Learning case studies circumnavigating the globe from Egypt to Australia. Part 2 illustrates Action Learning's scientific roots in studies of productivity and morale from coal mines, factories and schools. These studies from the late 1950s and early 1960s, based at the Manchester College of Science & Technology (later UMIST), also display Revans' even commitment to workers (or schoolchildren) and managers alike in his pursuit of improving the whole system of work.

In contrast to this operational research, Part 3 traces the historical, social and cultural context of Action Learning; the main theme being the long-established split between scholar and smith, artisan and scribe. A final perceptive chapter describes the future of Action Learning as worker participation in recapitulating the call for co-operation between the book and the tool. Part 4 prefigures the later *ABC* in setting out some the characteristics and logistics of the Action Learning approach.

The Origins and Growth of Action Learning (1982) Chartwell-Bratt, Bromley

> The "Collected Works" spanning the years from 1938 to 1981, its 52 papers running to 850 pages. The idea of Action Learning emerges as early as 1945 (in Paper 5 *A Staff College for the Mining Industry* p31), but many of these papers date from the 1960s and 1970s, with extraordinary bursts of output at the end of each of these decades.
>
> As Lessem points out in his introductory chapter, a clear biographical progression is apparent here, where "In trying to resolve the conflicts, dualities and paradoxes of his own personality, Revans has attempted to heal the schisms in his own society" (p5).

The ABC of Action Learning (1983) Chartwell-Bratt, Bromley

> Here are laid out the principles of action learning with P & Q, the Learning Equation, Puzzles & Problems, the Principle of Insufficient Mandate and many others. Although a first edition of *The ABC* appeared in 1978, and most of the chapters were pre-figured by the final part of *Action Learning: New Techniques for Managers* this is the fullest and also the most concise version of Revans' attempt to synthesise the essence of his idea.
>
> In contrast to, but building upon, the "scientific" view of Action Learning espoused in *Developing*

Effective Managers, here the emphasis is on human action, self-development and learning in sets and organizational contexts. This turn marks the result of twelve years' effort since the earlier publication, and constitutes Revans' contribution towards "a general theory of human action, for a science of praxeology".

OTHER PRINCIPAL BOOKS AND PAPERS

1. Revans R. W. (1949) *The Education of the Young Worker* Oxford Department of Education, Oxford University Press

2. Revans R. W. (1953) *Size and Morale,* Acton Society, London

   Based on the coal industry, this paper is amongst the first of his writings on the theme of "small is dutiful" and illustrating the damaging effects of large size upon communication, morale, accidents and productivity. The next paper below continues this theme with added evidence.

3. Revans R. W. (1958) "Human Relations, Management and Size" in Hugh-Jones E. M. (ed.) *Studies in Industrial Economics, Human Relations and Modern Management* North Holland Publishing Company, Amsterdam

4. Revans R. W. (1959) "The Hospital as an Organism" Paper presented to 6th Annual International Meeting of Institute of Management Sciences, Paris, September. The first of the hospital studies, involving five Lancashire hospitals, revealing the links between staff

stability and hospital communications on the one hand and length of patient stay and hospital waiting lists on the other. (Also Ch. 13 of *The Origins and Growth of Action Learning*)

5. Revans R. W. (1962) "The Hospital as a Human System" *Physics in Medicine & Biology* Vol. 7 October

6. Revans R. W. (1962) "Hospital Attitudes and Communications" *Sociological Review* No. 5 December

7. Revans R. W. (1963) "Management Education and the University Tradition" *Address to the CIOS Conference* New York, September

8. Revans R. W. (1964) "Bigness and Change" *New Society* Vol. 3 (66) 2 January (Also Ch. 13 of *The Origins and Growth of Action Learning*)

9. Revans R. W. (1964) *Standards for Morale: Cause and Effect in Hospitals*, Oxford University Press

   This first of three books on hospitals demonstrates that variability in communications, morale and patients' stay differs systematically by hospital and that variability *between* hospitals is greater than that within any one institution - showing that these are whole organizational characteristics.

10. Revans R. W. (1965) *Science and the Manager*, Macdonald, London
   A set of essays on sampling shop floor attitudes, technical knowledge, the pathology of automation, management control, industrial relations and

training which display a predominantly operational research orientation to organizational problems.

11. Revans R. W. (1966) *The Theory of Practice in Management*, Macdonald, London

    A set of essays on management education written in the first half of the 1960s. At this time of great expansion in the universities and in particular the establishment of the UK business schools at Manchester and London, Revans was unhappy with the existing diet of programmed management courses and proclaiming that the focus should be on helping managers *learn how to solve problems* (p5) and that the first need of the general manager is *to know the conditions under which persons, including himself, are able to learn* (p38).

12. Revans R. W. (1971) *Hospitals: Communication, Choice and Change*, Tavistock, London

    One of three books (two edited by Revans, one by Wieland and Leigh) on the Hospital Internal Communications (HIC) project 1965-1969 which, with its hundreds of doctors, nurses and other staff collaborating in ten hospitals, ranks with the Belgian Inter-Université Programme in demonstrating Action Learning in practice.

13. Revans R. W. (1976) *Action Learning in Hospitals*, McGraw-Hill, Maidenhead

14. Revans R. W. (1989) *The Golden Jubilee of Action Learning* Manchester Action Learning Exchange (MALEx), Manchester

A retrospective with chapters summarising the impact of action learning upon education, health and Third World problems, and a quantitative attempt to trace improvements in the Belgian economy.

15. Revans R.W. (1995) *Disclosing Doubts* First International Action Learning Mutual Collaboration Congress, April, The Revans Centre for Action Learning and Research, University of Salford, Salford

A further restrospective, covering similar ground to the earlier one and making an even more elaborate case for Belgian success being contingent upon the ability of "natural spontaneity". Here is Action Learning as driven by a sense of the limitations of learning, self-awareness and knowledge of the world, and of the need to frankly admit ignorance and seek fresh questions.

OTHER AUTHORS ON ACTION LEARNING AND RELATED APPROACHES

1. Wieland G. F. and Leigh H. (1971) *Changing Hospitals: A Report on the Hospital Internal Communications Project* Tavistock, London

The "official" report of one of the most comprehensive evaluations (although Revans elsewhere describes this as premature [1988 p33]) of Action Learning and the HIC Project. Revans' introductory chapter is notable for its emphasis on learning - on self-study and self-teaching as the basis for organizational learning.

2. Cortazzi D. and Roote S. (1975) *Illuminative Incident Analysis* McGraw-Hill, Maidenhead

   An imaginative approach to visualising problems and action learning situations by drawing them - another product of the HIC Project.

3. Casey D. and Pearce D. (1977) *More than Management Development: Action Learning at GEC*, Gower Press, Aldershot

   An important book of findings and experiences from the landmark effort at action learning in GEC which occasioned Revans' return to the UK in the mid-1970s. Also contains some participant accounts, including one chapter entitled "It didn't work for me".

4. Wieland G. F. and Bradford A. (1981) "An evaluation of the Hospital Internal Communications Project" in *Improving Health Care Management,* Health Administration Press, Ann Arbor, Michigan.

   In Chapter 24 of this wider work, Wieland revisits his earlier conclusions on the HIC and reports more positively on the effectiveness of Action Learning than he did ten years previously.

5. McGill I. and Beaty L. (1992) *Action Learning: A Practitioner's Guide*, Kogan Page, London.

   A useful book that takes a less Revans-centred approach and draws more on the traditions of group work. It is particularly good on the skills involved and also contains advice on how to run your own set without a facilitator.

6. Casey D. (1993) *Managing Learning in Organizations*, Open University Press, Milton Keynes

   Action Learning assumptions form an underlying perspective in this excellent and personal little book which includes chapters on working with teams, chief executives and the whole organization.

7. Dixon N. (1994) *The Organizational Learning Cycle*, McGraw-Hill, Maidenhead

   The author has brought together Argyris' action science with Revans' Action Learning and has pioneered the use of Action Learning in the USA. This book, reviewed by David Kolb as the best he had read on organizational learning, describes an organizational learning cycle parallel to the individual learning cycle.

8. Pedler M. J. Burgoyne J. G. and Boydell T. H. (1994) *A Manager's Guide to Self-development* (3rd edn) McGraw-Hill, Maidenhead

   Not focussed on Action Learning as such but embracing similar values, this is a comprehensive guide to management self-development designed to be friendly, challenging and action oriented.

9. Pedler M. J. (1996) *Action Learning for Managers*, Lemos & Crane, London

   A short, simple primer on how to do Action Learning with nine short chapters responding to key questions each containing ideas, resources and activities for practice.

10. Pedler M. J. Burgoyne J. G. and Boydell T. H. (1997) *The Learning Company: A Strategy for sustainable development* (2nd edn) McGraw-Hill, Maidenhead

   Attempts to realise the vision of learning community and learning company beyond the set of learning colleagues. Contains the Eleven Characteristics of the Learning Company and the Energy Flow model with glimpses of the Learning Company in action.

11. Pedler M. J. (Ed.) (1997) *Action Learning in Practice* (3rd edn) Gower, Aldershot

   A worldwide review of Action Learning practice with contributions from many of the leading practitioners.

12. Weinstein K. (1998) *Action Learning: A journey in discovery and development* Gower Press, Aldershot

   Previously published by HarperCollins (1995) this is distinguished by its attempt to give a primary voice to participants in describing and evaluating the Action Learning experience.

13. Dixon N. (1998) *Dialogue At Work* Lemos & Crane, London

   A review of writers on dialogue including Freire, Mezirow and Argyris, which discusses how talk can be made developmental in organizations.

14. Cunningham I. (1998) *The Wisdom of Strategic Learning* Gower Press, Aldershot

A confident, practical book which aims to bring about the "learning business" through "self-managed learning" - a methodology which has many connections with the Action Learning approach.

CONTACTS FOR FURTHER INFORMATION

The Revans Centre for Action Learning and Research is at the University of Salford. The Revans Centre offers research degrees linked to action learning and also holds the Revans' Archive of over 1,000 papers and numerous rare books. The Centre is a considerable resource for the development of Action Learning world wide, with international links with the USA, South Africa, Australia, Sweden, Belgium and Canada. Further information may be had from Dr David Botham, Director, at The Revans Centre for Action Learning and Research, Maxwell Building, University of Salford, Salford M5 4WT, England. (Telephone: +44(0)161-745 5718. Fax: +44(0)161-295 5494)

The International Foundation for Action Learning (IFAL) is an international network of people involved in Action Learning. IFAL is a registered educational charity, which maintains a library, a bibliography service, holds workshops, provides an advisory service, publishes a newsletter and otherwise disseminates information about Action Learning. It also has international links with The IFAL library alone contains some 800 items and a full list is available. Membership is open to individuals and organizations. Details from the secretary, Krystyna Weinstein at IFAL, 46 Carlton Road, London SW14 7RJ, England. (Telephone and Fax: +44(0)181-878 7358.)

Index

An invitation to keep in touch

To receive the latest information on forthcoming titles and developments in the Library please return this coupon to our London office at the address below. Also if you would like to comment on our books in any way, we would be happy to hear from you.

--✂

☐ Please include me on the Mike Pedler Library mailing list.

Mr/Ms/Mrs/Miss   First name _____

Surname _____

Position / Organization _____

Department _____

Address _____

_____

_____

Country _____

Postcode _____ Tel _____

Lemos&Crane
20 Pond Square
Highgate Village
London N6 6BA England
Tel: +44 (0)181 348 8263
Fax: +44(0)181 347 5740
E-mail: admin@lemos.demon.co.uk

A Concise Guide to the Learning Organization

Creating and developing learning organizations is an essential quest. But much of the available guidance is criticised for being long-winded and difficult to implement. Now, in *A Concise Guide to the Learning Organization*, **Dr Mike Pedler** and **Kath Aspinwall** show leaders and managers facing unprecedented and unpredictable change how to understand, embrace and harness practical principles, models and approaches that will enhance any organization's capacity to learn. Case examples and "snapshots" of organizations working towards learning are used throughout the book - as are activities that help you evaluate levels of development within your organization.

A Concise Guide to the Learning Organization gives you:

- a practical understanding of the nature of learning and organizational learning, and how the principles of the Eleven Characteristics of the Learning Company can be applied

- an appreciation of the blocks to learning, its limitations, and the shadow side of organizations

- ideas for future development - how learning organizations can contribute to the wider environment, their vital role in the creation of the Good Society.

Dr Mike Pedler, series editor of The Mike Pedler Library, is an adviser to some of Britain's leading companies, Revans Professorial Fellow at the University of Salford, visiting professor at the University of York, co-author of the best-selling *Managing Yourself, A Manager's Guide to Self-development* and *The Learning Company*. His co-author, **Kath Aspinwall**, is a lecturer in education management at Sheffield Hallam University and author (with Mike Pedler) of *Perfect plc?* and *Leading the Learning School*.

ISBN 1-898001-43-X

Also published in the Mike Pedler Library

Dialogue At Work

As much as 75 per cent of a manager's day is spent in conversation. Much practised but imperfectly understood, **Professor Dixon**'s book looks at the nature of talk and how it can be developed to form "dialogue". To manage change, complexity and diversity, organizations and individuals must develop. Individual learning has profound limitations. 'Doing dialogue' or 'development talk' in teams and groups is increasingly being seen as a new essential tool in managing change.

Dialogue At Work gives you:

- an understanding of the relationship between talk and development in organizations, how dialogue differs from the skilled talk that goes on all the time

- skills to recognise talk that hinders learning and development and means of rectifying this on an individual and group basis

- practical ideas to develop forums and conditions for dialogue based on research with leading companies

- summaries of leading theories on the nature and function of dialogue (Argyris, Bohm, Johnson and Johnson, Mezirow, Freire).

Professor Nancy M. Dixon is Associate Professor of Administrative Sciences at The George Washington University, Washington DC. She has served as a consultant to numerous companies including Unisys, Lockheed, General Electric Aircraft Engines, IBM, FAA, Whirlpool, Nippon Telegraph and Telephone Corporation, Japan. She is the acclaimed author of *The Organizational Learning Cycle*.

ISBN 1-898001-41-3

Resolving Conflicts in Organizations

Conflicts are common in organizations. Why do conflicts escalate? And how can they be resolved? **Dame Rennie Fritchie** and **Malcolm Leary** set out tried-and-tested approaches to help you understand the nature of conflicts in organizations and to implement strategies to resolve them. Working through the text with an example of conflict from your own experience, *Resolving Conflicts in Organizations* will give you:

- a framework to recognise the characteristics of a particular conflict - 'hot' or 'cold' - and how individual temperaments react to different kinds of conflict

- an understanding of how conflicts in groups can escalate - from discussion through to destruction

- the skills needed to resolve conflict at different levels of escalation through changing behaviour, attitude and perception.

Dame Rennie Fritchie's career has spanned insurance, industrial training boards, finance, consulting and health. For almost a decade she held chairing roles in the National Health Service and was a member of the National Policy Group. She is the author of *The Business of Assertiveness*. Her co-author **Malcolm Leary** is a consultant and researcher with many clients in the UK and throughout the world. He is the co-founder of Transform and a partner, along with Dame Rennie Fritchie, of The Conflict Challenge.

ISBN 1-898001-45-6